B TERRY ECKERSLEY **ornReady**

"He's a tonic" – J.John

"Inspirational" – Surrey advertiser

British Library Cataloguing in Publication Data

A catalogue record for this book is available from the
British Library

ISBN: 978-1-907636-59-2

Design, Typesetting and Print Management by Verité CM Ltd

Printed in the UK

Contents

Commendations

Terry is a remarkable man who has achieved an extraordinary amount. Yet as he admits in his candid account of his life, all that he has done is because of a God who, through his astonishing grace, rescued him out from life's depths and changed him completely. The fact that God can transform a man like Terry today greatly encourages me in sharing the gospel: may Terry's story similarly inspire you!'
Revd Canon J.John

Terry is a very special person, he is a trophy of God's grace, love and mercy. His Amazing story serves as an example of how God turns losers into winners!

This book is a recipe for success!
**Rev Davey Falcus, Lakeshore Ministries, Real Deal Plus.
Author of Gangland To God**

A searingly candid and compelling account of a harrowing young life rescued by God's grace. Terry spares nothing, least of all himself, in describing the nihilistic destructiveness seducing U.K. youth and in unforgettable prose he presents the Answer, allowing the reader to experience self-discovery with laser-like clarity. A valuable addition to my library and it will be to yours too.
Rabbi Daniel Lapin, President, American Alliance of Jews and Christians

I have known Terry for nearly 14 years. I first met him early in 1999 when I turned up in Sheffield to commence my registrar post in pathology, and Just as Terry was very single minded in his old life, of sex, drugs and rock'n'roll, in his new life as a christian, he was equally determined, and never had the television or internet at home, and would spend his time regularly praying, fasting and watching christian teaching DVD's; I believe this choice of pursuing 'sanctification' and God, would form the foundation for the restoration from his old life, and later his success in both his marriage and career.

The well known evangelist, J John describes Terry as a 'tonic'. There are many other unique aspects to this man, which I ought to mention. He is skilled in the ability to encourage, and bring people Terry is a living testimony to the grace of God; how He takes a delinquent teenager from the suburbs of Lancashire, and uses him for His glory. It's been both an inspiration, and a privilege to see how the Lord has worked in his life, and those around him. Despite knowing rich and famous people, Terry has always had time for his old buddies from Sheffield, and I can testify that he is a loyal friend. At age 51, at the time of writing this, Terry seems to have more enthusiasm and energy than ever, and I'm sure that the best is yet to come.

Dr Nick Tiffin, Consultant Pathologist

I have had the pleasure of knowing Terry for over 20 years! Warm, positive and incredibly humorous are just a few of many superlatives that come to mind. I have personally seen Terry develop and prosper in ways most would not believe and against all odds. His qualifications and achievements are an inspiration to all who know him. He is a true friend and one who always encourages without criticism. I can honestly say Terry is a friend for life."

Wayne Leigh, MD, Jott Europe
(Wayne worked with Terry at Think media Music)

Terry is one of the most enthusiastic and energetic people I know. He is an amazing guy who has an incredible story and it's not over yet!

Jeff Lestz, Co-CEO Genistar, Financial Education & services

Terry is brilliant businessmen with a very sharp mind. When it comes to marketing, managing, brand awareness and all around business acumen Terry stands head and shoulders above the rest. Terry does this by maintaining good ethical practices and bringing an unparalleled level of integrity and wisdom to all that he does."

Dayle Rodriguez, Artist, Think Media Music
(Dayle worked directly with Terry at Think media Music)

Terry Eckersley is one of the most inspiring people I have ever met.

His guidance support and knowledge is second to none. He does not judge but cares, he is generous with his time and commitment to his colleagues. His networking skills are unbelievable.

He has a natural aura about him and a charisma that makes you want him to be a part of your working day on your team – "He's a top bloke"

Maggie Naylor, Development Officer, YMCA
(Maggie worked directly with Terry at Woking YMCA)

Terry continues to be an inspiration to many. His work ethic, heart and passion for those that he works with is unmatched. A transforming character and positive outlook mean Terrys work will always create a longterm impact on all those that he comes in contact with especially with those at Woking YMCA. Highly recommended." May 12, 2011

Joe Clark, Project Manager, Hillsong London
(Joe was with another company when working with Terry at Woking YMCA)

Terry is a very knowledgeable and helpful individual who will put himself out to help others. His enthusiasm and character makes him the sort of person you want in your team. I have enjoyed working with Terry in the past and would certainly work with him again in the future."

Bob Riley, Lecturer Brooklands College

(Bob worked directly with Terry at Woking YMCA)

One of the difficult things in business is to understrand the real motive and agenda that lies beneath the surface of people. What I love about Terry is that his confident engaging approach, efficient management skills and superior leadership abilty are all delivered with a genuine, caring and passionate heart."

Steve Rolls, Director, Douglas & Rolls Financial Planning Ltd

Introduction

Terry has come a long way from his humble and tragic beginnings. His dad died at 13, this hurt and angry boy rebelled into the care of the local authority. He soon got lost in the drugs and crime of the council estate in greater Manchester. He progressed to drug addiction and crime and finally prison, the cycle continued until he found salvation in Jesus Christ. A powerful conversion led to a mighty healing experience, he then forged a career in the Church and YMCA helping others.

The Queen invited him to one of her garden parties for the work he had done via the YMCA in Surrey, starting from scratch to over 10 centres and 300 staff.

Against all odds, Terry has academically achieved a professional diploma in housing, Post Graduate Certificate and Diploma in Business Administration. Also a natural and humorous Evangelist both one on one to large conference crowds he shares his story and the Gospel. He has had many challenges to overcome even a potential lawsuit from Steve Jobs and The Apple Computer and Phone Goliath. Some call him a social Entrepreneur, some a media mogul having his music placed on BBC, ITV, SKY serving TV audiences and TV & Radio via www.thinkmediamusic.com

Humorous and engaging, Terry has a unique gift with wide reach that impacts lives forever. Coaching business and Charity CEOs to greater success is a service Terry also enjoys.

He relaxes swimming, walking and spending time with his family and forever sweetheart Jill.

Now also in demand consulting and fulfilling speaking engagements, you can't put him in a box!

Foreword

Thanks for taking time to read and share the story of my life, thus far. Yes, it can be deemed tragic, yes, it can be deemed sad, and exciting, and up and down, and sometimes glamourous. Yes, I have made many mistakes in my life, I'm sure I've made many mistakes recalling my story, so please forgive me in advance. I only want to help.

I have overcome my difficult at times and lonely and tragic childhood, it wasn't all bad I did have a family who loved me as best they could. Humour has been a tonic, so has faith and faithful friends. There is something in here for everyone, yes, even you.

I have overcome many addictions, and heartaches and seemed to bounce back, time and time and time again. Maybe I can help you? I think we all have had lonely and dark times filled with glimmers and sometimes full beams of sunlight lighting up our whole world, countenance and the world around us. I hope this book can help push back any darkness in your life. Be encouraged, you too can bounce back. I believe in you.

This is a book of new beginnings, hope, success and love, the wonder of love. You may laugh, cry, get sad even angry, then move on into the victory I have found and continue to find. Keep seeking and you will find.

I hope and pray you find encouragement from this story that includes many stories of battles, fights, and some amazing coups. I am a very fortunate man, that could help unlock fortune in your life. Please, let's be friends now, and feel free to connect with me as we can navigate through this huge journey called life. Why is it called life? Because my friend, as I have learned, it's for living!

Terry

From humble beginnings. Had to restrain me even then!

CHAPTER 1

Unexpected Beginings

*"I'm just a man, not a hero.
Just a boy, who wants to sing this song."*

GERARD WAY

Born ready; ready for a decade later to be christened 'the swinging 60s', at a time when Britain was poised for massive sociological change. I arrived at a time when the Conservative government was in the twilight of its thirteen-year rule, soon to be rocked by scandal and controversy. 'Johnny Remember Me' by John Leyton rang out from radios and juke boxes across the land, a No 1 soundtrack for my inauspicious debut. It was the year Bob Dylan relocated to New York and visited the gravely ill Woody Guthrie in hospital. Dylan vowed to keep Guthrie's leftist humanitarian agenda alive. Guthrie was also a major influence in the life of Joe Strummer of The Clash, the only band that mattered to me as I grew up in the 70s.

I was born in a working-class area of Greater Manchester, a place called Leigh, in Lancashire, on a council estate called Higher Folds. It was one of those estates almost built away from everyone else, separated by fields, woods meadows and the slag heaps – these were mountainous terrain for a young boy. As I recall this, the estate seemed in black, white and grey, as did the slag heaps. Made of a grey type of shale, it was the unusable material from the local mines. I actually made my entrance on the sofa of our semi-detached council house in Royal Drive on September 17th 1961. The youngest of five children, my brothers (Jimmy and

John) and my sisters (Patricia and Irene) had all left home apart from Pat, by the time I was born. I was the unexpected child, and I really felt like the unwelcome one; my earliest memories are of feeling like an orphan at times.

Higher Folds was very much a working-class estate which was gradually becoming deprived. It was typical of many similar estates of the early 1960s. The majority of the people who lived on the estate were decent working class people, predominantly miners and cotton mill workers. Over the next decade it was to become more of a giro estate (this was the unemployment cheque you cashed at the post office). As miners' strikes, pit closures and the decline of the cotton industry hit the area hard, innovative and illegal entrepreneurs began to rise up. And later on, I would become one of them.

As I've mentioned, Higher Folds was surrounded by slag heaps, or 'rucks' as we used to call them, residues of the once-thriving mining industry in the area. Brooks of water used to run down from the rucks and there were fields and meadows and woods beyond, where I was to spend my early years playing and exploring with my friends. When I say exploring, we would go climbing trees and bird nesting, collecting wild birds' eggs. We also used to play soldiers in the trees and meadows.

My father was Roman Catholic; my mother converted to Catholicism to marry him. Roman Catholicism was just part of the way things were to me as a child. I went to a Roman Catholic school and a Roman Catholic church. I was baptised in a Roman Catholic church and grew up in a Catholic household and accepted what I was told. I imagined God as an angry old man who would beat me if I did wrong. It seemed it was just a lot of ceremony and rules and regulations.

My mother was a real character: she used to work on a bread van and she worked on a fruit and veg stall on the market, so she knew how to talk and shout and bring up five kids! She was very loud and a lot of people, in fact everyone, knew her and some were quite scared of her. My father was a gentle type – he was a local miner, eventually achieving fifty-one years' service. He worked night shifts and consequently I saw little of him, just at breakfast times and weekends and on holidays. He loved music and was always singing songs to himself, particularly Jim Reeves' songs, like 'I Love You Because You Understand Me' and 'The Old Rugged Cross'. I have great memories of my loving Father, putting me on his knee and singing to me.

On a hill far away stood an old rugged cross,
the emblem of suffering and shame;
and I love that old cross where the dearest and best
for a world of lost sinners was slain.

(Refrain:)
So I'll cherish the old rugged cross,
till my trophies at last I lay down;
I will cling to the old rugged cross,
and exchange it some day for a crown.

O that old rugged cross, so despised by the world,
has a wondrous attraction for me;
for the dear Lamb of God left his glory above
to bear it to dark Calvary.

In that old rugged cross, stained with blood so divine,
a wondrous beauty I see,
for 'twas on that old cross Jesus suffered and died,
to pardon and sanctify me.

To that old rugged cross I will ever be true,
its shame and reproach gladly bear;
then he'll call me some day to my home far away,
where his glory forever I'll share.

Lyrics and Music: George Bennard, 1873-1958

This beautiful song with its powerful words and symphonic melody, really moved me, yet I didn't yet understand the old rugged cross.

Strangely, in view of the path my life was to take later, he called me 'Lazarus'. Lazarus was a person in the Bible who died and was raised from the dead by Jesus. In many ways my life was to be raised from the dead. I was very much dead at certain stages in my life. I don't know why my father called me this, but it was certainly prophetic.

We had a front garden and a back garden. My father was a keen gardener; he used to plant vegetables in the back garden and flowers in the front. He was such a kind guy he used to do a lot of other people's gardens as well. I didn't have many toys – I remember making a lot of them myself, with my dad's help, making wooden swords and trucks made out of old pram wheels which I used to play with outside. I also made toys indoors: garages made out of old shoe boxes, aeroplanes. We had one of those front rooms which you only went in at Christmas-time; we more or less lived in the smaller back room. We had two coal fires (we got cheap coal as my dad worked down the mines). I always ate sitting on the floor as we only sat up to table on Sundays after we got back from church. We would then have mats on the table and be sort of 'posh' as we ate our Sunday dinner, but the rest of the week I used to eat off a plate on a newspaper tray. My parents also used to use chip trays and mince pie containers as ashtrays. As I said, innovation due to lack was acceptable.

Television played a big part in my life. I used to watch Crossroads when I came home from school, and I liked programmes like Top of the Pops and Coronation Street. I always watched the news and Look North, a local ITV news show. Anthony H. Wilson, aka Tony Wilson, had a big interest in music. He'd interview bands and then they would play – bands like Slaughter and The Dogs, The Buzzcocks, and all the other emerging punk bands. These bands would often then play at Anthony H. Wilson's first venue The Russell Club, which became The Factory, and yes, that's where Factory Records got its name from, or vice versa. I got to see lots of amazing bands when I was seventeen and eighteen: Siouxsie and the Banshees, The Ramones, Iggy Pop, Adam Ant when he was underground and had a cult following, all dressed in black, Ant Music for sex people. Of course Adam went on to have huge success with the MTV revolution that started. His videos, always flamboyant, were perfectly suited to MTV.

When I was small, I was always sent up to bed immediately after Coronation Street – 'up the dancers' was the term we used for going upstairs to bed. My home life must have been much like my peers' at this time: watching television with my mother, reading and playing with my toys in the evenings. Sunday nights were always 'bath nights' in those days – in the downstairs sink when I was small, and upstairs in the bathroom when I was bigger. I did all the usual stalling for more time to watch TV, but almost secretly I loved going to bed.

My bedroom was called a box room, any clues why? Exactly, it was the room over the stairs and was very box like. This was much more than sleeping in a box though: I had my own secret world, my own magical world. It was filled with Aesop's fables, the Brer Rabbit books, Famous Five. I had to enter these secret worlds via another secret world – a torch, a book and hiding under the bed linen.

I do remember having old Bry-Nylon sheets and pillow cases and old blankets although I did have a real eider-down duvet. I never went cold. Everything was old and grandparents-ish. I sought solace with my books and dictionary. I always used to look up words I didn't understand, so I got a real good grasp of the English language from an early age. I was mainly self taught, like more things I will share with you later.

I had four main words growing up: why, when, where, and what for? I was always told off for it by my mum. She would say, '"Why, when, where, what for?" That's what we should have called you.' It feels strange now looking back at having a mum who didn't want me to ask questions, broaden my horizons. 'Sit down and be quiet. Your tea will nearly be ready,' as though this would answer all of life's questions. Underneath this hard exterior she had almost a contradictive, oxymoronic caring heart. She would talk to anybody and always have a laugh and a joke. I remember mum would shop for neighbours who couldn't get out much, and even take a lady out in a wheelchair. Wow, that's selfless, hey?

I went to a junior school called St Gabriel's. I really liked school. My parents didn't take me to school, my mum and dad were working. Geoffrey Hurst and Christopher Cook were responsible for taking me to school and bringing me home; they were well-respected local boys a few years older than me. The headmaster was called Edward Roach, a very dignified, well-spoken gentleman, always full of joy and love. He used to get us all singing along with him at assembly in the mornings. I was selected for a group of about six highly-gifted children to prepare for the 11 Plus exam. This was an exam that decided if you got into Grammar school or not. I was a bit of a character from the start always having fun and devouring the books in the library. Then I'd have to go on to the next class up, to start on their books. I really excelled in English. Unfortunately, although I was part of the group who had special tuition for their 11 Plus examination, I never passed it. I was a borderline decision, so I was told, and I was sent to St Mary's School.

At my junior school I remember one incident when I was jumping on a hosepipe – I got the leather strap for doing this. This was to be the start of quite a long-standing discipline in my life, capital punishment it was called. It involved being beaten with a strap or being hit across the hands with a cane. They beat and caned me so hard that my hands would swell up and blister. This was something that really confused me. I was crying out for love, support and acceptance, and all I seemed to get was six of the best.

I also started my career as an altar boy, being a Roman Catholic. I remember making sins up when I went to confession, because I couldn't remember doing anything wrong. This was all to change in later years! Recently I met up with three old school friends: two I went to secondary school with, and Micheal Doyle, who I went to primary and secondary school with. We are organising a school reunion. Micheal reminded me that we used to have a little tipple of the communion wine! I don't remember this, and apparently it got us the sack. The priest put a pen mark on the level and we were caught! Bang to rights. This was all interesting as the priest thought I had great potential to be a priest! I didn't fancy it. The thought of not having a wife scared me, even at such a young age; I wanted a wife and family.

The church was St Gabriel's. I was an altar boy there as my two brothers James and John had been. It was very quiet and austere there. The Giles brothers, Peter and Andrew, were also altar boys at the same time as me. One of the Giles brothers went on to become a policeman and our 'careers' did cross once or twice! In later years, Mum, Dad and I used to go to church every Sunday morning; we used to have a brunch when we came home. It was the done thing to go to church.

My sister Patricia used to look out for me. She encouraged my mum to buy me good clothes as Mum was content for me to wear clothes from older family members. Mum also used to buy clothes two sizes too big. 'He'll grow into them,' was often said at the clothing store, even when we were getting a free school uniform. My sister encouraged

Mum to buy me fashionable clothes; I suppose she didn't want me going through the ridicule and shame she went through. Pat insisted on me getting decent clothes and going to a proper barber instead of mum cutting my hair with a big pair of rusty carpet scissors and a basin. It wasn't all poverty and doom and gloom though. I have memories of coming home from the market where mum worked on Saturday afternoons – I used to be sat on the back of the fruit and veg van going home with the wind blowing through my designer bowl-and-carpet-scissors haircut. I really enjoyed this, so did Mum and it was extra cash for the household.

When I was a young boy, about six, I remember getting a bicycle for Christmas, a small one with stabilisers. I went to my auntie's house daily with my mum and all the family congregated there. Auntie Lily was like a grandmother figure – we'd eat traditional Lancashire food like stews and broths. Auntie Lily was the stereotypical Lancashire battle-axe, large and muscly, curlers and headscarf. Contrary to the way she looked, she was loving; loving to me and the family and food! Aunties, uncles, brothers, sisters all met at Auntie Lily's. It was a real centre of love and family. The family would all shop around for bargains and buy them for each other, all done with good heart and fun and banter. And then one day, I went there on my own on this little bike. I was missing and everyone was looking for me, the police were notified! I went all that distance (Auntie Lily lived about four miles away in the town centre). Eventually I was found when Auntie Lily took me home. So looking back, even as a young boy I was a bit of an adventurer. Would this lead to great adventures later in life? My bike was confiscated, but that didn't stop me – I set off on foot and started to walk to my auntie's. I was shown love and care there so that's where I headed. It's that simple; we go and stay where we get love, care and respect.

I remember another occasion, years later, when I was

about twenty years old. I went round to Aunt Lily's one night, and they were having a séance about one of my cousins who was going through a divorce or something – I walked in and it absolutely freaked me out. All the family were sat around the table holding hands, the room was eerie and ice cold and Auntie Lily was asking questions and getting messages from the other side! Nothing else was scaring me at that time in my life. I said to my mum: 'Mum the priest would be very upset if he found out about this,' and I just ran, terrified, away home. I had some sense of the supernatural and I didn't like the vibe I felt.

As a family we always went on holiday twice a year, two weeks in June and one week in September ('we' being my mum, dad and myself. Notice who always comes first – Mum! She really did wear the trousers in our household, and looked very good in them! No really, Lancashire women seemed to live on a diet conducive to big bellies and large frames, sorry girls. My dad was tall, lean, always smiling and always wore a suit when not at work. We made things together like cars out of old pram wheels, chassis, seats with carpet, axles and a rope steering wheel. 'If you ever do anything, do it well,' was my dad's advice. We had great fun making these and then playing in them. Me and my friends would push each other in turns on our very own Brands Hatch! In later years I started to recycle bicycles with old bikes we found dumped in the local fields. I would take the good parts and clean them up with Brillo pads to get the rust off. I'd then buy new cow horn handle bars and paint to re-paint the bicycle frames, selling them after a short time of use. Then I progressed onto motor bikes which I would then ride on the fields and scrap heaps, which was very much like a Motocross track. It was perfect for pulling wheelies and doing jumps.

We went to Blackpool every September to see the

illuminations amongst other things, they just happened to be turned on. Mum loved the bingo. I would always be begging for more money from Mum for the slots. I found it boring in there playing bingo and, as Dad would say, there was always only one winner. We also spent time on the beach and donkeys. Great fun. We always went to the south of England for our two week holiday: places like Bognor Regis, Torquay and Newquay, usually at holiday camps. I loved the times on the beach. I loved swimming in the sea, and still do; I find it exhilarating. It seems to blow away all the cares and worries of life, allowing the waves to crash against me. Playing games with the waves, waiting until the last minute and then running until, as the waves would catch me up, I would get swept off my feet – again on a magical mystery tour where the wave would take me.

Life was very much the same routine, day in day out, week in week out, months, years. Mum and Dad always seemed to have petty arguments. Dad would say, 'You'd take the goodness out of anything!' (this was when he was eating), and Mum would start nagging him. I can't remember what she was asking him or talking about. Mum was a very strong character and seemed to always be having a go at him, although they would soon make up and did really love each other. I can picture them walking hand in hand on the coastal seafronts of our holidays. Don't forget they'd already brought up four older children, who now all had kids of their own, one older than me. It did always seem strange, like I was getting brought up by grandparents. I know they did try their best but I never had a birthday party or cake! As a child, I never got taken to school or had any encouragement with my homework or at any sports days. I was really lonely. Dad was either working or sleeping; Mum was also working. I was lonely and alone on my own in our house.

I had some unconventional pets as a child, firstly a

magpie which I hand-reared when I was eleven years old and a polecat named Prowler when I was twelve. I used to take Prowler to rabbit holes with a snare. This was not very successful – we never even caught a rabbit. Once Prowler went down a rabbit hole and didn't come back out. Three weeks later I heard that a local farmer had found him, and went to see him and got him back. I was very angry with the farmer's son for keeping my pet. I used to take him out for runs on a local football pitch and have so much fun. But I don't remember what happened to him after that. There was a rabbiting culture on the estate, so I was trying to get in on that. Stereotypical Northerners, hey, flat caps and whippets. I also bought an air pistol and an air rifle and we used to go shooting birds and rabbits. I was a very good shot with birds, however I never got close enough to any rabbits! And the pellets would have probably bounced off – I only had a .177 and then, later, a .22 air rifle. I really started to like guns. I am a good shot and I liked everything about guns, the cold steel, the wooden butt and also the power I felt when I was in possession of any firearm. I also had a pet kestrel. I did a deal with one of the older guys at school who had stolen two kestrels out of a nest; I had one and another friend had the other one. I used to keep it hidden in a box because I couldn't keep it at home. Somebody found out where I had hidden it and stole it. I found out about this and remember giving the guy a bop on the nose. I was very angry! He was a stocky young guy but this just didn't seem to bother me.

When I was thirteen I bought a tawny owl off somebody and kept it in our shed, but it fell ill and died. As I mentioned I also did a lot of bird-nesting, stealing birds' eggs, which was the prevailing country mentality although we lived on the outskirts of a big city. My first pet after my birds was a whippet which I had for just one day. I got it from a friend at school but my mother made me take it back the next day – much to my upset and embarrassment – after it yelped and howled all night. I was very lonely and a dog would have been an ideal companion.

Whilst at junior school I endured my first life-threatening experience (more were to follow later in my life). I had my appendix taken out when I was nine. I was at home on the sofa (or couch as we called it) suffering from stomach pain for about a week. My mum told me to lie down and relax, but I was in agony. Little was I to know that my appendix had burst. The pain continued and my mum took me to the doctors on the bus to see our family doctor, Dr Stone. He sent us straight down to the hospital. We walked down to the hospital, and I was taken straight into the operating theatre. I had the appendix taken out and also had a tube fitted for all the poison to drip out. After the operation the matron found me walking to the toilet on my own, which I shouldn't have done. She went crazy at me. Here I was wondering around the hospital in the middle of the night. This was the beginnings of this fearless, adventurous spirit which was to take a wrong turn later in my life.

I left my first school at age eleven, ready to start my secondary Roman Catholic school, St Mary's. What would this have in store for me? I remember getting a free school uniform and free dinner tickets, which was all embarrassingly undertaken, but hey, they were given out. Shopping with Mum was fun, like I said earlier she would always get me things far too big. 'He'll grow into them,' she would say. My blazer was like a Crombie or trench coat and my shoes, well I took two steps forward and then I would move; 'put some paper in the toes' – we certainly had a poverty mentality, deeply engrained.

Anyway the first chapter of my life was over at St Gabriel's School, my Roman Catholic school on the council estate. I was now moving to St Mary's Secondary Modern School. I did feel genuinely excited about this new prospect of moving on and meeting new friends at my new school.

On the step again. What a cutie!

Family time at Blackpool Pleasure Beach

Look at those knees!

Holidays. Hello ducky!

My mum at home in Leigh,
Greater Manchester UK

Terry training to swim for
Lancashire! Greater Manchester UK.

Look at those knees!

School photo. What a handsome
young man!

CHAPTER 2

St Mary's School, My Family And Music

"Let's keep the car in drive and leave it all behind"

JOHN MAYER

I had just failed the 11 Plus and went to St Mary's Secondary School. We had all our old friends from junior school, but there seemed to be loads more children and I started to settle in quickly and meet new friends. I met another Eckersley there, Paul Eckersley, and John Simmons was my friend. His nickname was Jibbs and we hit it off. He has since told me his parents were as old as mine were and I don't think he felt or got much love either.

The pranks Jibbs did were very funny, simple things like making loud squeaking noises and keeping a straight face whilst the teacher would get increasingly annoyed. He also made up names for people so Michael Doyle, my friend from St Gabriel's, would become Sir Arthur Conan Boiled Egg! A long connection from the Doyle to Boil but somehow this made it funnier. I also made up similar names and, looking back, we were trying to be intellectual, whilst showing very little interest in the subjects. Many teachers and students became our study and fun, often leading to discipline. We were caned across the hands, bruised, beaten – looking back on this I am sure this was abuse. I always got six of the best which was three lashes with a cane across each hand! The headmaster, heads of year or departments would mete out this discipline. The games teacher or PE teacher would also give us the cane for simply not excelling in sports activities! It was during one of these disciplines that

I got whacked across my wrists which swelled up really badly. On this occasion it was my friend Roy Pickering and I. Roy only had one arm – he was a thalidomide child. Pregnant women in the early 60s could take the drug thalidomide to prevent morning sickness. A side effect was many children were born with a lack of limbs. Another girl in our year had two very small arms. Her name was Anne and she was always smiling and insisted on doing everything for herself!

Anyway, I was enjoying school, having fun. I was starting to become a bit of a class clown, I think, in fact becoming a lot of a class clown. My reports always said I did very, very well, lots of potential in me, but needed to be the centre of attention. But looking back I think it was because I wasn't getting any attention anywhere else, and the only attention I could get was by performing. I met up recently with my friend Jibbs who reminded me that I would impersonate other school friends and even make songs up about them and sing them. Would I do anything with these skills later in life?

At this time, music began to play an important part in my life. The radio was on all the time at home, and music was a constant part of my childhood. The music of the 60s was a soundtrack to my life in my first ten years, then the music of the 1970s for the next ten years, which coincided with going on to secondary school. I loved The Beatles and other rock and roll bands in the 1960s. I also liked the music coming out in the 1970s, all the glam rock like Slade, Sweet, Mott the Hoople. I remember hearing 'Roll Away the Stone' at the local fairground just blasting out. This song really moved me and through such a powerful sound system, with the lights as well, it was just so powerful. I remember on one of our holidays hearing a song playing through the sound system. It was David Bowie's 'Life on Mars'. Wow! I was transfixed by this music and lyrics.

I was to become a real Bowie freak – I was given a David Bowie (and a Motown Gold) album for Christmas when I was eleven or twelve, together with my first record player, which was a massive deal for me. I had my hair cut spiky like David Bowie had at the time.

The cinema or 'movies' was a big part of everyone's life back in the 60s and 70s. We used to go to the picture house opposite Leigh Market every Saturday lunchtime. That was the market my mum worked on every Saturday as well as working on a bread van every day. It was quite funny: we knew and described people by what bread they had – 'You know Mrs Smith who has two toasties and bread cakes at weekends? Well, her sister's auntie's died!' It was all very much Peter Kay type observational humour living.

It was a fun upbringing, and we did find a lot of humour in who we were and what we did.

Anyway… the movies. It cost sixpence to get in, if we paid. Most times we climbed through a window round the back and sneaked to our seats. Flash Gordon's Trip to Mars and other serials were shown but, strangely enough, neither he nor any other film characters were heroes to me. Maybe that was something that was lacking for me as a child – I didn't have anyone to look up to. I didn't have ambition, or any role models, we just seemed to get on with it, life.

Smoking was another part of growing up. It seemed that virtually every adult on the estate smoked. My father smoked Woodbines, quite a lot of them, and I started smoking around the age of eleven. I used to smoke behind the bike sheds at St Mary's School; that was the place where everybody else smoked. We thought we were cool if we smoked, blew smoke rings, and could do a trick with a box of matches! I could flip the box sending it spinning into the air, catch it, and the match would be lit. Then I would coolly, or more like a young plonker, light my cigarettes!

I was very small and skinny at this time. I was never

keen on sports and I never used to get picked for football teams as I was a bit of a weakling. I would always be one of the last to be picked. I was much smaller and skinnier in stature than my contemporaries, and I seemed to have two left feet! When I was at junior school I always got picked, played rugby and cricket, but all these guys from other schools were like grown men! Massive, some with moustaches, beards, hairy chests! I had ribs like a toast rack, sparrow legs and had to run around in circles to get wet in the shower. We used to go on cross country runs, although I used to avoid them whenever I could. PE and sports were not a big thing in my life, and I remember getting the cane because of this. I was keen on swimming though, and was such a strong swimmer that I was chosen for trials for Lancashire, but never got the opportunity to show exactly how good I was, as I got caught smoking on the balcony at the swimming pool. Consequently I was caned and banned from taking part competitively in the only sport at which I excelled.

When we went swimming my mother would give me old towels full of holes, much to my sister Pat's embarrassment. Pat, who always looked out for me, gave me a really nice big bath towel to take to the swimming baths. My mum took it off me and put it away in a cupboard and gave me one of the old ones instead! An older woman known to the family used to take me to the baths from around the age of ten, and I used to stay over at her house after our swimming sessions. This was to lead to a situation which went on for over a year – an older woman encouraging me to touch her sexually in return for money and sweets. This must have had some kind of effect on me, although I don't remember feeling at all guilty or disturbed by it at the time. She treated me well; bought me sweets and gifts. She also locked me in a trunk suitcase and laundry box, this scared and confused me and I have had to constantly forgive and push against confined spaces.

I came home from school one day, thirteen years of age, to an event that was to actually rock my world. Some school friends came running towards me saying 'Shall we tell him, shall we not?' Looking really concerned, they were reticent to tell me something that would change my life forever.

'Shall we tell him, shall we not?' The puzzling words rang out. I stood confused as my friends looked at me in consternation. Then one of them told me that my dad had died. It was my father who had shown me love, affirmation and encouragement. He was a tall, gangly man who always had a smile on his face. He was always happy and seemed to enjoy his life, working regular night shifts at the local coal mine. I only saw him briefly during the week, in the mornings when he got home from work, and at weekends when we all went to church together and had a full English breakfast when we got home.

I'd been looking forward to spending a lot of time with him because he was retiring – I was thirteen and he was sixty-six – and he had suddenly died. When I went into my house my mum hugged me and cried; it was the first time she'd ever hugged me, and it was the first time I'd seen her cry. Mum was a typical northern working-class woman, she didn't show much emotion. She was outgoing, jokey, yet could get quite angry. She was very popular and everybody seemed to know her. When she told me my dad had died I didn't cry and I wasn't to cry for the next fifteen years. I went up to my room and slammed the door to my room and the door to my heart. I vowed no-one would ever hurt me again. Life wasn't fair, I felt cheated and abandoned, hurt, lonely, angry. Why had God let this happen? Why had he been taken from me? I felt numb, dazed, but most of all angry. That was it – the young Terry Eckersley started to become hard-hearted. I wasn't going to let anyone close to me again. I remember going back to school and just really not caring any more. I went from being a bit of a class clown to just completely not caring.

I was obviously given time off school. The funeral came around very, very quickly; I was still in a state of shock, and very angry. What struck me about the funeral was that Dad's body was in the house, laid in the coffin in the front room of our house. And then we went to St Gabriel's Church, which Dad had always gone to and where I had been an altar boy. Rather than our usual friendly walk, it was different this time. We went in big posh limousines, which were posh to me. Would this be the only time in my life when I would drive in a big posh car? Anyway, we went to the cemetery which was a few miles away. It was huge, filled with lots of old grave stones and new ones. Everybody was upset and sombre. It seemed nobody knew what to say to me. Why did it have to be this way? Why could I not have a normal family? Why were my parents not younger and encouraging? And now my loving dad was gone. It was true, the man who always smiled at me, encouraged me, sang and joked with me, my hero was gone forever.

I felt lonely, hurt, scared. Words were said, sand was thrown on the coffin, the grave was then filled in. And I just felt myself getting more angry and angry, harder and harder; and more of the resolve came into my heart that no-one was going to hurt me again. I wasn't going to let anyone in my life. It just felt so unfair, because the only person who showed me any love and firmly encouraged me was now gone forever. The words on the headstone read '*A lifes work well done*'. It just didn't seem fair, I was heartbroken. A life's work well done? He had fifty-one years' service down the local coal mine, retired, then died all within a few weeks. All the sacrificial night shifts, noble as they were, to bring extra money into the family home seemed in vain. I would never become a miner; this would never happen to a family of mine, if I ever had one.

I didn't seem to have the inspiration to study. I was hurt and angry. I saw no counsellors, no support. The whole school seemed to know that my dad had died when I got back to school. Teachers said they were sorry, the other kids didn't know how to react – neither did I. I was in a sort of daze. I couldn't engage, my attitude had changed significantly. I started not doing what I was told. My mum was equally angry and I kept getting shouted at. Then my mum got a couple of the family men to punish me. I'll knock it into you; I'll beat it into you. I didn't know what 'it' was but the beatings hurt and again seemed unfair. Wham, the sting as my relative's hand hit my face; slap, on the other side of my face, both rocked my head violently side to side. Behave yourself. Do what you're told. Are you listening? was being yelled hysterically at me. I smelled the alcohol on my relative's breath as he seemed to enjoy beating this thirteen-year-old boy.

Confused I tried to calm him down and explain. Don't answer me back. Shut up. Don't make me more angry. I was really confused, I was hurting on the inside and now I was hurting on the outside. I then did answer back, screamed back, leave me alone, stop it! He responded with harder beatings. The real reason he was angry was because his wife had left him to bring the kids up on his own, and he'd been beaten up by his wife's new lover. Hurt people hurt people, they say, and he certainly did.

There didn't seem to be anyone there who could just listen to me, or talk to me, or give me any love or encouragement – I'd just get beaten. It was the same at school; you'd just get the cane. There wasn't anyone there to sensitively listen or encourage, or understand; people just wanted to give you a good hiding. That was all I got from anyone: a good hiding from my family, and the cane from the authorities. All the time. And in a way, in the end, you just stop caring about it and I think quite a part of it was I pushed them as far as they could go. No matter what they threw at me, I just kept bouncing back and bouncing back, and bouncing back and bouncing back. I think I developed a resilience and tenacity in those early years, when I just kept getting up and getting up and getting up – that's all I would do.

How could I live in this environment? I couldn't. I ran away from home at thirteen. I slept rough or I was sneaked in to friends' houses. It felt good not being constantly put down and beaten. Eventually the police caught me and I was locked in a police cell. My mum then came to get me, even more angry as she had been made by the police to come and get me. This meant a family drinking party would have been disturbed. I was the blame for everything, I was useless, I was a hindrance to my own family. I often thought that this wasn't my real family, that Id been adopted. Why did I get no love and support? Why did my dad die? I would sleep at night now in a foetal position, lonely, scared and angry. I didn't want to read anymore.

My sister Pat, though, was always still sticking up for me and being kind. She had married a cool guy, a builder called Raymond, nicknamed Jas. They had bought an old house and refurbished it, sold it and bought the one next door and did the same. I was always made welcome there. They had a red E-Type Jag sports car and sometimes I would get taken for a ride in it. 'Jump in kid,' she'd say. Wow, this was exhilarating and I felt really cool! We really stood out in our neighbourhood in this kind of car.

I'll introduce you to the rest of my family.

My eldest sister is Irene and she's about nineteen years older than me. Irene left home and went to nursing school in England and directly after finishing training she went to America and did very, very well in nursing. My memory of Irene is that she used to come home and bring great gifts for all the family. She was like a real Mother Christmas, not

Father Christmas. One Christmas she bought me a blue Chopper bike. To have a Raleigh Chopper bike was like, wow, you've won the lottery. I think I was the only person in the whole of Leigh who had a Chopper bike – one of the first anyway; and it was a real, real deal. And Irene used to do that, buy us all gifts. Interestingly enough I later led her to have a real, living Christian faith. She has a daughter called Amy, and is married. I'll tell you about the Christian faith stuff in a short time... keep reading! I went over to see her in America after she had a triple heart by-pass operation in the 2010s some time. It was fuelled by my concern for her, and my desire to get a close friend, Sean Parry, off heroin and prescribed opiates addiction. (Again, I'm getting ahead of myself . . . stay tuned for how I got mixed up in this murky world of sex, drugs, crime, prison and hopelessness.) I thought Irene's situation was more serious than it was and when I got over there she seemed more fit than I was! She came bouncing all over the hotel room, full of life. America was an amazing place. We visited New York, the Empire State Building, Broadway, Grand Central Station. Wow, America was amazing and a long way from my council estate in Greater Manchester beginnings. I'll explain how I got from one to the other, hold on tight!

My eldest brother is a guy called John and he's seventeen years older than me. He lives in Leigh and is married to Teresa and has five children: John-Paul, David, Yvonne, James and Janice. He spent most of his life working at BICC (British Industrial Calendar Cables) except when he was younger he was a bit of a lad, a bit of a hard nut, pardon the pun. He used to be known for sticking his nut on people. A bit of a hard guy that people knew was not to be messed around with. He loved his rock and roll music and was a great fan of Buddy Holly. I used to go and stay with them some weekends at their home in Glebe Street in Leigh. Fond memories.

His daughter Yvonne and her husband Phil were helping to nurse my dying mother years later when I was working at Sheffield YMCA. I was starting to get my act together but it was a 'knives could cut the air' scenario. John-Paul's wife was with them and I remember there was a bit of an atmosphere. This was because years before, when I was in my early twenties, I got blamed for something I didn't do: stealing a video recorder from my nephew John-Paul. I hadn't done it. When you are a drug addict you do get the blame for all kinds of things – you also get away with a lot! This accusation had led to a fight with his brother David that I did not want, but felt forced into. He was developing a reputation as a rugby fan thug and got charged for it. We had a good old scrap and I beat him. As it was escalating into greater family feuds, my mum stepped in. So, we just didn't speak for years. I apologised for my part in the family conflict, what I'd not been and not done and for what I had done. This built a bridge with Yvonne and Phil. We became good friends and all of us are very supportive of each other. Phil, Yvonne's husband, had a private chat with me in his car later that day. He said it took a real man to apologise, and we had a good talk. He was pleased that I had humbled myself and asked for forgiveness. I really respect Phil and honour him for that and, in later years, I was able to help him through some very difficult situations. It's a good story of conflict and reconciliation that had come about because of my new life and faith that demands, in a loving way, reconciliation and forgiveness. I believed God had prompted my niece to care for her dying grandma (my mum), as I had cast my cares on him. 'Humble yourselves, therefore, under God's mighty hand, that he may lift you up in due time. Cast all your anxiety on him because he cares for you' (1 Peter 5:6,7).

Unfortunately since then Phil and Yvonne have divorced and that side of the family once again is in tatters.

My other brother is Jimmy who is sixteen years older than me. He spent his life bringing up four kids and in later years took up window cleaning which he was still doing until recently. And he still lives in Leigh, bless him. He's a real character, just like Mum really, just like Irene and myself. Nothing seems to get him down; he's always got a smile on his face.

And then my youngest sister Pat who's twelve years older than me. My memories of Pat are that she was young, trendy, had sports cars (two E-Type Jags). I used to spend time going around to their house, chilling out, listening to music – I loved the music… well, that's Patricia Eckersley.

It was my sister Pat who encouraged Mum to buy me a record player. (A record player was like a big box with big speakers. In the middle of the big box you put a record, a single track or LP – long playing – with many tracks on.) I also got two LPs: Motown Gold and The Rise and Fall of Ziggy Stardust and the Spiders From Mars. Wow, wow, wow, I had found a new world of love, a new world I could escape to. I heard about love on the Motown album, all the greats: Marvin Gaye, Diana Ross and the Supremes, songs like 'What Becomes of the Brokenhearted'. People knew how I felt and they expressed it in their songs. 'What Becomes of the Brokenhearted' was a favourite. It was a question I was also asking but getting no answers. But then I started to get an answer, 'Why Don't You Build Me Up Buttercup?', 'Love train', happy, upbeat songs. This became my new world for a while, the back room, playing my songs. I did get the occasional 'Turn that down!' It was like I wasn't allowed to enjoy life, always spoken to harshly. I started not to give a crap! Oops, did I swear? No, it stands for 'carefully read and processed'.

David Bowie took me to his world, another planet and he took me there via rock and roll and other music. He sang of Lady Stardust and Ziggy Stardust, which was really him! Songs with great mental imagery.

I'd also found a new group of friends at school. These friends, like me, all had one thing in common: we were hurting, bad, deeply. My new bunch of friends included Roy Pickering and Paul Eckersley. Roy Pickering was a thalidomide child who had a plastic arm, long hair, a real tattoo – not the home-made ones we did with Indian ink and sewing needles, Roy had a big peacock tattooed on his arm. He also had the burden that his parents were split up and his mum had cancer! Paul Eckersley's dad drank too much and beat him regularly. We started to 'wag' school – play truant. Roy would take the suppressor caps of his mum's car, and when she went to work on the bus, Roy would take us out for the day. We also used to go on shop-lifting competitions, to Manchester and Bolton. Paul Eckersley – remember, not related – started to steal money from home. So we became the best-dressed, best-fed kids in our town. We started to live life like we wanted, how we wanted, with who we wanted. I know, this sounds like the beginning of a real crazy roller coaster ride! Hold on tight!

Enjoying a family holiday in
Blackpool with mum and dad

CHAPTER 3

Further Education, Attendance Centre

*"Hey you, don't tell me there's no hope at all.
Together we stand, divided we fall."*

PINK FLOYD

I started playing truant more and more. We unconsciously formed a school gang. All of us were having problems at home: cancer, divorce, death, alcoholism. My friend Paul Eckersley (no relation) who was being beaten by his father and going through his parents' divorce used to steal from his parents and we started to go truanting together. Paul was much different to me in many ways. He was a little shorter but quite stocky, with red, tight, curly hair. We seemed to click from the word go. We were in the same class and having the same name helped, I suppose. Paul later went down the Hell's Angel route, and also became a hard core drug addict like Roy Pickering and myself. We really didn't seem to get any supportive help or counselling, just beaten with canes.

Paul bought me lots of new clothes which I'd wear to go to our local cities, Manchester and Bolton. Paul used to steal the money from his dad's pockets as he lay asleep after one of his drunken nights out, when he'd come in and give Paul, his mum and three other kids a hard time. I used to call for Paul. He lived near the old bus station at Leigh, right in the town centre in an old terraced house. I always waited for him in the back garden. They had a big, white pit bull terrier which looked very scary but was very friendly. You know what they say about dogs and owners? Well, this pit bull did remind me of Paul's dad, who I rarely saw. Angry-looking, thick set, ready for a fight!

Paul then encouraged me to try and steal some money from home. He told me of some hiding places. I checked and wow! I found a wallet with lots of crisp cash in it.

And so I started stealing from my mother. We used to play truant, regularly. Wagging it, we called it, although quite sophisticated, we thought! We always wrote our sick notes and took them in from our parents. This was my first dabble at forgery, writing a sick note to my form teacher and forging my mum's signature! I was good at this and never got caught playing truant! We also stole clothes from outside shops. I didn't have many clothes, so I used to tell my mum that people were selling them at school because they were too big for them. I'd get the money and the clothes, so it was another bit of a scam.

When I came home from school (or wagging it) there was no one there for me. There would be a note on the fireplace (just like the Oasis song): 'Dinner on plate in micro oven. Put on for three and a half minutes, love Mum.' Not microwave – we call ours at home now a 'micro oven' in memory, and laugh about it.

I was all alone, getting no help or support, only beatings, which soon stopped as I started to stand up for myself. My uncle would come around to our house and beat me and beat me and all this was in the presence of my mum. I remember barricading myself in a bedroom, so scared and trying to protect myself. He was knocking some sense into me: 'I'll teach you a lesson, be good for your mum.' I'd smell the alcohol on his breath. He was a very angry man, my uncle, always angry about anything. He later developed rheumatoid arthritis, which I believe (and research shows) is medically linked to unforgiveness and bitterness.

It wasn't all bad though. I remember school with fondness, I met some great friends there, not all of them got into trouble. I also remember the Queen's Silver Jubilee. We all went to the East Lancashire Road from school to watch the Queen drive past and wave. Would I ever be in Her Majesty's company again, or at her pleasure? I really didn't have a clue about the future. The Sex Pistols released 'God Save the Queen' that year, in a mocking way. And on their first album they covered an Iggy Pop song, 'No Fun', and sang of 'no future' in 'God save the Queen'. Those words seemed to prophesy over many of our lives.

I also met up with all the other rebellious people who were going through a lot of hurt and pain. Roy Pickering was a character. Although he only had one arm he could drive better than anyone I knew, chat the girls up better and fight better. When I say he could drive better, he used to take the compressor caps off his mum's car so she couldn't start it. She'd have to go to work on the bus and we could then steal the car and go joy-riding in it. We were all about thirteen or fourteen years old.

At this time in my life we were shoplifting all the time – we'd have shoplifting competitions in Manchester. We'd steal things for ourselves and things we could sell. For example yo-yos were in fashion, so I took orders for them; we'd steal watches out of cupboards in shops; I stole a load of car keys from a car supplies shop and then we could steal out of cars.

Then we discovered motorbikes. We'd buy old motorbikes – it started off with a little moped scooter and then progressed to a Honda 175 CB (we used to go out on the fields on that). The biggest I got was a Triumph 350 for a short while. This of course developed into more when I stole the Vauxhall Viva when I was thirteen. I drove to Manchester and through to Liverpool with pillows on the driver's seat so that I could sit on them and see over the steering wheel. This brought excitement into my lonely, hurt and angry young life. I didn't even think about any consequences. When you have nothing left to lose, or it seems that way, you take many risks and life-threatening decisions! This was to put my own life on the line and, sadly, other people's, time and time again as I got older. Later coming back onto the estate we were seen by my friend's brother who told his dad, and the police. So there you go; my first car-stealing expedition. We went and got arrested for that and I don't think I stole any cars after that

I first ran away from home around this time. I was thirteen and I slept on friends' floors after they smuggled me in at night. We then started getting caught for shoplifting, Roy stealing his mum's car, we just went crazy. In the end, Roy's dad wouldn't have him home and my mum wouldn't have me home; we were too much trouble and embarrassment. So Roy and myself, rather than get bail like our co-defendants and friends, we got sent to an assessment centre at Atherton. This was like a massive school full of unruly young guys, up to age sixteen, I'd say. The rest of the population was all from around Manchester and Liverpool and everywhere in between. It was quite intimidating on arrival. Our possessions and clothes were taken; then we showered, were seen by the doctor and then sent to our dormitory. I didn't really feel anything. The place was clean, the food was good. I soon settled in. I really enjoyed getting stuck into the schoolwork. The teachers seemed amazed at my grasp of English and my art really excelled. Woodend, as it was called, wasn't a bad place. Just one or two of the teachers would really lay into (beat-up) some of the other boys. I had made a decision: I was going to keep my nose clean, and I did. We were there for three weeks. Roy and Paul got care orders, put in the care of the local authority. I was given a chance – I got my two years' probation.

I went home and back to school. I was like a local celebrity now, everybody wanted to know what it had been like. I settled back in well. If I went on a more intense therapeutic programme, I could get the probation cut down to a year, so I did. I enjoyed it. There were about five of us on this programme. We did everything from play darts, pool or chess together, to going away on barge trips. I'm sure we did all the teamwork and leadership skills on these trips away. I remember them being fun, and the probation officers were very caring and supportive. And to be honest this did keep me out of trouble from thirteen to eighteen years of age. Despite my celebrity status at school I managed to keep out of trouble with the police. We used to spend time in the youth club which is at the bottom of Stirling Close where my brother Jimmy lived. He was around forty-five years of age and divorced. His wife left him for another guy and he was left to bring up the children, John, James, Katherine and Tony, on his own. And they have all fantastically turned out really, really well. My nephew James went into the Army which did him the world of good. When he eventually got out he was qualified to drive Big Trucks, so that's what he did. So did Tony but without the Army in-between. John got an apprenticeship in a garage, and that's what he does to this day, only now happily married with four kids of his own and settled in Australia!

I remember going to the job centre just before I left school. They asked me a few questions, then made their minds up. A labouring job, that's what you can do. I got no other options. OK I had left school a.s.a.p., but was there nothing else?

CHAPTER 4

Leaving School, Starting Work and Detention Centre

"You're an expert at sorry and keeping the lines blurry"

TAYLOR SWIFT

I left school at sixteen years of age and started cleaning windows. All I did was look in the local paper under 'Jobs', saw the window cleaning job advertised, went to the red phone box at the top of our street at the side of the bus stop (both smelled of urine), I rang the guy, had a telephone interview and I got the job straight away! Wow! I was really happy about the thought of working and making some money. I really enjoyed the guy I worked for and I got paid a decent wage at the end of the week. I paid my mum £10 per week and the rest was mine.

I started to go to the pubs around town on the weekends with friends from the estate. Life was balanced and sensible. I was very quick cleaning windows, I always did them well. I used to save time by putting my ladder in between two upstairs windows and moving it along with one foot on the wall and the other on the ladder. I would also slide down the ladder!

At this time Warrington New Town was being built; all new houses and industrial estates. Well, we canvassed all the work and I helped build up a very big round. I got on with my bosses, recruited a couple of other guys to help with the work, and if I worked Saturday mornings my boss let me keep all the takings for the work I did (thanks, Pete, if you're reading this). It's good to be generous and reward hard work. I did that for about a year, making money and spending it, chatting girls up, dancing, drinking, using cannabis which we bought in anything from £1 wraps to eighth and quarter ounces. We would use what is now called 'skunk' which was simply weed, dried cannabis.

Although when I was a window cleaner I really enjoyed going to Manchester town centre and picking the most trendy, slightly expensive attire, we would also look at all the music, and the new music coming out. Bowie was still top of my list, with Iggy Pop and Lou Reed. We thought we were the coolest cookies in town. My hair was like Bowie's at the time: side parting, long fringe, short back and sides. And, as I said, the Punk revolution started, wow! This was very cool, exciting, it explained how we all felt – angry – and a way to get it out was by pogo-ing, jumping up and down. The energy level was so raw. So raw, in fact, that I started having time off work and then went on the dole. I was in the Punk scene and lived in many different places; girls' bedrooms were the best, but if there was no joy there, friends' houses. I slept one night in a skip full of cardboard! I was so drunk and too exhausted to walk home. That was one thing about my mum, she did love me the best way she could and I always had a bed there.

The Punk scene was very exciting. There was a bunch of us on the estate that all became punks – David Fairhurst, David Shovelton, Tony Prescott, Colin Reynolds. I became good friends with Colin; we both could sort of play the guitar, but his brother Alan, wow! He could play Dire Straits' 'Sultans of Swing' like Mark Knopfler. To hear him was a real inspiration and treat.

I jumped fully into the fast moving river called Punk and we went to Manchester to see all the Punk bands: The Damned, Adam Ant before he became commercial, The Ramones, Siouxsie and the Banshees, Iggy Pop. I really did see all the amazing new bands in this revolution called Punk.

We had to fight through the streets of Moss Side Manchester ghetto to see the bands, that's how determined we were. The venue was the Russell Club, which then changed its name to The Factory after factory records, and the driving force Anthony H. Wilson who I had the pleasure of meeting once. He was with the tongue in cheek Punk hit, 'Jilted John' by Jilted John! I took the Punk movement very seriously and the political and social comment in Strummer's lyrics were the Gospel of Punk to me. It wasn't something commercial to make money from the youth. A line in the song 'White Man in Hammersmith Palais' says, 'You've got Burton suits, you think it's funny, turning rebellion into money.' This was aimed at the suits The Jam were wearing. This was a dichotomy Joe always had to battle with as The Clash achieved great success, therefore money, even though he did do a double album for the price of one and then a treble! Joe became a hero of mine, who I was later to meet at The Leadmill in Sheffield when I was completely different man. I was also to meet the original Clash drummer Terry Chimes in London and take him for lunch, giving him advice about getting a book published, as I was later to have success with a book. But hang on… I don't want to jump the gun!

We had to fight past black gangs, then dance to Reggae music together – punky reggae party. Bob Marley was a great track and sentiment and I did feel a minority, just like blacks did back then. Peter Tosh, from the Wailers, Steel Pulse a Rasta band from Birmingham, and lots of dub reggae were played. I love the track Joe Strummer and The Clash wrote after Joe went to the Hammersmith Palais. We bought resin and ash – then the pub scene came along. The Sex Pistols, The Clash, Slaughter and The Dogs. I got involved in that.

I first ran away from home when I was thirteen and left home again when I was eighteen, living in cars, living in a shed, and then got sent to a detention centre. This was for a scam in arcades. I could use a bit of wire, and voila! I could empty the machines, cash as well. They were bound to find out because, talk about thick as thieves, I didn't even go to different arcades or amusement parks to repeat the scam. I went back and back to the same one and eventually got caught. Again, I went through the process I was used to as a boy, and I was off for a taxi ride handcuffed to two police officers, taking the scenic journey to Rochdale.

Detention centres were part of the government's drive with the short, sharp, shock treatment! I got taken to Buckley Hall Detention Centre in Rochdale. I went there with a sort of excitement and fear. I went through the whole process of putting my Punk attire into a box in exchange for the general prison uniform: cheap-looking denim jeans, a couple of T-shits, vests, underpants (Y-fronts in fact) and slip-on black leather shoes, not the height of fashion but good quality leather shoes. I always got bought 'pleather' as a kid. We then got taken in an escorted police van to Buckley Hall Detention Centre – we being the new recruits. I use this term because I was going to be army trained, whether I liked it or not!

Part of the initiation was that when you were in your cell for the first night, all the other inmates would bang and scream abuse through your door, trying to scare the new recruits as much as they could. I was fortunate as the other two new recruits came from a heavily publicised case at the time. They had been involved in witchcraft and tortured and sacrificed animals to Satan. Cats! So these two guys got loads of abuse about this. 'Cat killers, cat killers,' everyone screamed as they came and went to evening classes. 'Meow, meow, hiss, hiss,' everyone taunted them.

The next morning we were taken to our respective dormitories, to place our kit and start our induction. It was a three-month sentence, but you did two months then you got an EDR, which stands for 'earliest date of release'.

Why was it not called an EDOR then? I never asked!

We were taught how to make our bed, in a special way of presentation. There was also a way of folding your kit, all very neat. The sheets were cotton and the blankets were nice and warm. I was clean, and managed to get on with the other inmates. I didn't enjoy the gym; imagine how unhealthy I must have been. Remember I was so skinny I had to run round in the shower to get wet! If I wore red I got mistaken for a thermometer! But seriously, we had circuit training army drill style. Guys would throw up regularly or collapse. I was very fortunate not to. If you got caught cheating, for example doing ten press-ups instead of twenty, the gym instructor, who was an officer too, screamed at you, sergeant major style: 'Come on you pansy, you horrible little man. Think you're hard now, do you? We'll get you in shape, and everyone else another twenty star jumps because of you, Eckersley!' Star jumps are jumping up and down and making a star shape with your arms and legs. The gym was set up with weights, ropes and benches. You followed around the circuit and at each point it was written on a card how many and what you had to do. We did get good demonstrations beforehand.

Anyway, I got very fit, very fast – I had no choice. We were taught to march, go on parade, be inspected outside in the courtyard and inside about our personal space. Again, if there was the slightest thing out of place, you got screamed at and your kit scattered across the dormitory. I learned to become tidy and organised, very quickly. Everyone worked during the day. We all started on cleaning floors, scrubbing them, wiping them down, polishing them. I thought the food, which we ate in a big dining hall, was great, and I struck up some good friendships in there. It was mainly through similar interests – my main love was music, and I connected well with people around this subject.

I had been a singer in a band we'd set up before my sentence. I wrote one song, it was called 'Looking For Fun'. I won't bore or excite you with the lyrics yet but, keep going, could something special happen with this song? You will get to find out later. We didn't get a gig or even try. We practised a bit, but mainly we enjoyed smoking the weed, so that's what we would end up doing.

This sentence was for stealing money again, another step in education towards crime, meeting lots more inner-city kids who thought it was almost a noble profession to become a criminal. So that's what I came out of it all wanting to be – a young criminal. I came out and carried on in a career of crime. I started burgling shops; met a girl who worked in a bank and got her stealing from the bank. Owning a car and motorbike became my ultimate goals. And then I got introduced to heroin and Diconal. I also started carrying a switch blade dagger around with me for protection.

Diconal is a synthetic opiate and I became addicted to it. I suppose it just comforted me. I felt loved and warm. I remember my first injection, preparing the fix, crushing the tablets, putting the powder into the syringe, adding water, then finding a vein and drawing in some blood to make sure – then, bang, injection, and the most amazing feeling of euphoria! It was orgasmic. It was pure feeling and all the pain went. The hurt of my dad's early death, the loneliness, the beatings – this seemed the answer. The cannabis use was more of a peer, cool thing to do. I smoked it all the time and it did make the opiate buzz last longer. I'd first tried cannabis when I was a window cleaner and going out for the weekends. I could buy more than I needed, sell some of it on and get mine free, make some money. By now I had progressed to buying & selling substantial amounts of cannabis resin allegedly. This, I thought gave me money, power, leadership and kudos. I'd get drunk, take downers,

Valium and barbiturates. My girlfriend at the time worked in a chemist and I got her to steal these, under the guidance of a local Hell's Angel. His name was Colby and he had long red hair, oil-covered jeans, leathers and patches. He also had a hunch back. I liked him, we got along well and he loved the Punk scene and music. I also got into amphetamine, chalkies at first. These where slimming tablets but, boy, did they give you a buzz. I took these and ran in the fast lane of The Clash first album. I was hanging around all the other local towns now, seeing bands, taking drugs. I became a real hardcore Punk: dressed that way, lived that way. It was exciting, yet lonely; bright and rebellious, yet very angry.

As I said, I got caught for ripping off the fruit machines in an arcade we used to frequent. I had a public order offence for breach of the peace in Bolton, this was between Punk Rockers and Teddy Boys! I know, how silly and childish. That's what lots of alcohol did to me, I wasn't violent, really?

Well for the foolishness and charges above I got the three months detention centre I was telling you about – short, sharp, shock!

CHAPTER 5

Drugs And Rock 'n' Roll

"A pill to make you numb,
A pill to make you dumb
A pill to make you anybody else,
But all the drugs in this world
Won't save her from herself"

MARILYN MANSON

Ian Dury and the Blockheads had a song out called 'Sex & Drugs & Rock & Roll' which fitted the story of my life very well. It was the theme tune for this period of my life, and many others around our area and similar areas in the UK.

Opiates, heroin, Diconal made me feel warm, comforted and healed. I fell in love with the only love I had ever known. It was deathly, dangerous, yet it took all the pain away. The only way to get it was through regular criminal activities and from doctors, legally and illegally. Meanwhile I had been building up a hefty Crown Court appearance list with various drug related crimes and shop burglary, we even tried to get the safe out of a local Co-op store! We were crazy, but whilst mooching around the back of the largest department store in the town centre, we noticed one of the back doors had been left open! This was like letting kids loose in a sweet shop, well the sweet shop part of the mall or supermarket these days!

We were out of our heads on downers, or benzodiazepines, and alcohol. It was more disorganised crime than organised. We started filling bags up with watches, but this was a department store, if we'd have been in a fit state and thought this out properly, well, we could have started to empty the place. It also had a bank on the top floor. I had a brainwave. We got some tools from the DIY department, and slid under the bank tellers' serving hatches, and started to try and saw through the Co-op Bank's safe! We took turns at sawing and chiselling like crazy, sweat dripping of us. We were trying to saw through the hinges of the old safe and were getting closer and closer! This could be the big one, all by a flukey chance. One of the team left with his bag of swag – watches, jewellery, etc. – he was the wise one; we carried on and on. Anyway, the top man of the store, the boss, remembered he had not locked this door and came back! Suddenly, looking directly at us were the police, loads of them, some in uniform, some plain clothes. 'Come on then,' they pleaded, they couldn't get through the tellers' windows. (I told you I was skinny!) So me and my friend Neil ran away and hid in an old dusty room at the back of the department store.

We sat there; we must have looked a sight, hiding with all the clothing dummies! All dummies together! We could hear the police and the dogs.

'They're gonna find us,' I whispered as I heard the dogs, this is what they're trained for. Right then, we made a decision: let's make a run for it. So we started creeping out of the darkened room, onto the back fire exit.

'Here they are!' a policeman yelled.

Off we ran. Now opposite the Co-op on this lovely summer's evening were all the locals cheering us on as we ran as fast as we could; it was very Keystone Cop-ish. The entertainment that night was on us: everyone was cheering and laughing as we kept running. It was no good – we were unfit drug addicts, they were fit healthy policemen with dogs: do the maths, they caught us.

They put us in the police van and took us to the police station. As soon as the doors opened again I was off, running as fast as I could. I got about a quarter of a mile away, chest burning, getting more and more out of breath. I was caught, again! This time they handcuffed me. I was taken back to the police station and bailed. The rumour went around that we had been caught whilst posing as dummies in the shop window!

At this time I had got talking to a beautiful blonde woman who was my age and worked in a bank. I managed to chat her up and we started dating. This was probably my second serious relationship. Her name was Debbie and she lived in the next town although she stayed over at our house a lot. We did have a good relationship, looking back; we had fun, shared musical tastes, and we smoked dope together. I was still mad for Diconal, or any other opiate when there were none around. You guessed it – she devised an elaborate system to steal money for us, to buy drugs and so that I could play the big shot. This money was in crisp £50 notes and it kept us going until I had to appear at Manchester Crown Court. We were expecting borstal training, and welcomed it; it was another progression in my educational training and the family I was now part of.

The day soon came along and I stood, with two co-accused, for the Co-op bank burglary and some other minor misdemeanours. The prosecution presented the case and our barrister used some mitigation, but in those days it was the norm: we all got sentenced to borstal training, six months to two years. If you kept your head down, you got out in nine months. Sounds weird but I didn't care and was determined to enjoy this journey. We got taken down to the holding cells and, that night, all three of us went to Strangeways – David Fairhurst, Neil McCullough and myself.

Strangeways was and still is a massive old prison, just outside the centre of Manchester. It was very imposing with big gates, to go through. We were then led into reception and started to go through the process I'd got used to every time I'd got arrested: name, date of birth, medical examination, shower and then into the prison uniform. We were then led up to the Prison wing. Strangeways had a young offenders' side, a remand side and a convicted prisoners side. We were led onto the centre. This was a big metal sort of octagon shaped iron, in the centre and then about six wings came off this. A wing was like a block of flats only cells, four stories high and separated in the middle by a toilet and slopping out area. Yes, slopping out was a process after meals where you put your trays that you had got one of your three meals a day on, and it was an opportunity to empty your slop buckets. Yes, again, these were buckets that you had to use as a toilet. You could press your buzzer and if one of HMP officers were around they would let you use the toilet – this was understood as if you wanted to sit down, otherwise you could urinate in your bucket!

Anyway, I had been to Strangeways before for twenty-one days when I was about nineteen for non-payment of a fine, so it wasn't as intimidating as it was the first time. Walk with a swagger, keep smiling and joking; only the weak ones got made fun of or picked on.

David and I went to our cell together. That's another thing, in most cells there were two beds, either bunk beds or two beds separated by a cupboard in the middle. But there were also some single cells and some with a bunk and another bed: three people to a small cell, with only buckets for toilets, but hey, this was prison. David and I ended up getting allocated to an open borstal and Neil went on to a closed borstal, just down the road from where we lived. Neil was the guy I stole my first car with. He had an athletic build and was a nice guy. He got a job as gym orderly at borstal and when he came out managed to play professional rugby for the local team, Leigh. He also got a job and he wasn't interested in the crime or drugs anymore, for which we all really respected him. Like another associate of mine John

Pendlebury. He did some petty crime with us but he ended up playing for St Helen's Rugby League and then went on to coaching. Both these guys never got in trouble again.

I don't remember withdrawing much from the drugs on this occasion, we hadn't really become hardcore users or addicts by then. Once, twice, three times a week, not a day!

My sentence was from six months to two years. Most people are given time back when their behaviour is good and they've worked with the programme. Time would be given back after our meal one day when everyone was in the huge dining hall. I remember on my first review period, which was like an assessment, I lost time because I thought my borstal training was a big joke. This is what the senior officer told me. This was an unusual occurrence, most people were given time back, or not given time back, to have your earliest release date was almost unheard of, but so was the style of Terry Eckersley.

It wasn't so much as I thought it was a big joke, I just used to stay upbeat and have a laugh, use my humour to get through the day. But I must admit that I did have a bad attitude towards authority.

I decided to learn guitar in borstal, primary chords, notes which I still know to this day. I found it amazing that all the best songs, well a lot of popular songs, had been written with these chords. I learned G first and then I kept strumming that chord, over and over. I then learned E and again kept strumming that over and over. Then I put the two chords together and would strum away to G and E. I learned a Jam song with just these two chords. Paul Weller had written the song 'That's Entertainment' which was a tongue-in-cheek look into the UK in the late seventies and early eighties.

I liked The Jam, but not as much as The Clash. They were both classed as Punk bands but although very good and politically charged, Weller's songs didn't seem as raw and real as the words and lyrics of Joe Strummer and Mick Jones of The Clash. I was now starting to get some heroes, like these musicians; I never in a million years thought that I would ever get to meet them

I got on well with the other guys in borstal. I loved the whole 'Rock Against Racism', that the Punk and Reggae bands moved forwards. I also loved the Reggae music and it was natural for me to get on well with the black guys in prison situations or in everyday life. I felt we had so much in common through music, and I also felt like a minority, although not ethnic but still a minority of the working class that it seemed were destined to labouring jobs, the dole, unemployment benefit, or crime!

So borstal was like a university of crime: you heard what the other guys did, got tips, got ideas. Then again, I didn't really want to reform. I met some interesting characters, inner-city guys. I wanted to be like them, they seemed to know ways of making very easy money, having a good lifestyle. And as Joe Strummer sang in the track 'Bank Robber', a lifetime behind one machine, is ten times worse than prison. I related to this, it came back to my dad's death – fifty-one years' service down the coal mine then two certificates: one for service, the other a death certificate. I remember going to a church meeting where I said to the Christian visitors that Jesus doesn't like the bankers either, he turned the tables over. I suppose I was trying to justify my way of life.

Before I went to borstal a significant thing happened. I was in a friend's house; his dad had gone away, so we'd been taking drugs, sleeping with our girlfriends. This friend of mine started reading out of an occult book, and this particular evening lots of weird, crazy stuff started happening. I started seeing things – manifestations – and it wasn't just the drugs. It really, really freaked me out. This was after I had gone home terrified, I hadn't been taking magic mushrooms or LSD or any other hallucinogenic drugs. A friend of mine, David Shovelton, was freaked out – he came knocking on my door – we were both freaked out. Up until this time nothing scared me at all, man nor beast, but I was terrified. My mum told me God was warning me.

David had also been seeing and hearing crazy things. I saw demons and some huge frog-like things. I saw into the spiritual realm for the first time!

> Then I saw three impure spirits that looked like frogs; they came out of the mouth of the dragon, out of the mouth of the beast and out of the mouth of the false prophet.
> (Revelation 16:13)

David came and knocked on my door and said, 'Has it been happening to you, too?' He looked terrified as I said, 'Yes!' Just then there were almighty screams coming from somewhere. They didn't sound like humans or animals; we were very scared! My friend and I went to a local preacher who used to preach to all the Punks outside the local shops and the local night clubs. I just admired his courage and boldness and I was respectful towards him, partly because I had been brought up in a Roman Catholic church, was an altar boy, attended Roman Catholic schools, but mostly because of his boldness, his lack of fear and bold faith. It was dangerous out there; there were often fights, police and ambulances. Yet here he was with a friend – they both had bibles and would be telling anyone who stopped that Jesus loved them so much he had died for them. I listened, asked questions, and he befriended one of the most crazy and getting dangerous young men, around town – me! We called him Stan, Stan the Preacher Man.

David and I went to Stan – in fact we ran as fast as we could to Stan's house. He was in bed but got dressed and welcomed us in. We told him the whole story and he told us we were messing around with the devil and that God loved us and that Jesus died so that he could break the pattern. And he asked did we want to give our lives to Christ? Were we sorry for all that we had done wrong?

At that moment if he had asked me to jump through hoops of fire backwards I would have done that, but there and then, David and myself got down on our knees in his front room and asked Jesus to forgive us and gave our lives to Christ in the most sincere and best way, we knew how. I felt a little something happen, but not a great deal. I realised what I had done, but I didn't understand what Jesus had done.

David went on to become committed to a church, got a job and was doing well for a while. He looked so well and healthy. He worked at a dentists' suppliers for a while, where he had access to syringes and all sorts of things we could use. However we didn't ask him to do anything for us in that way. Anyway, he truly was a changed man, looking and living healthily, attending church. He also started to tell people now about Jesus, just like Stan. I was pleased for him, but I wasn't fully ready yet. I just thought there was no way I could be committed to a church and, to be honest, just didn't want it.

Later, many years later, at Stan the Man's house, when someone else had moved in, I heard Bob Dylan's 'Mr Tambourine Man' which had a profound spiritual effect on me. This was because I first gave my life to Jesus in that home and the next time in there this song was playing, it was as though God was the great tambourine man, and Dylan, you, me are asking him to play a song for us, and in our own jingle jangle way, we will go following him.

CHAPTER 6

Borstal Training And Escapades In-Between

"Emancipate yourselves from mental slavery.
None but ourselves can free our minds."

BOB MARLEY

I got allocated a great job in borstal! Joking… I was digging trenches, digging trenches. This was after being allocated a job in the kitchen where they put me on potato peeling! I tried my best but catering for so many people was no easy task, so I refused to work and got marched down the block (this was the punishment wing: solitary confinement, one hour's exercise, walking around in circles). The next day I had to see the Governor. I lost another week's time and was kept down the block for a few days before going back up on the wing.

I did have a big attitude problem with authority. Authority had always put me down, beat me. It had never encouraged or affirmed me.

I soon started to understand the system and got sick of digging trenches! I realised the futility of my rebellion; it was making life very hard, mainly for me!

I decided to take the chip of my shoulder, stop playing jack the lad, start being respectful to the warders. They started to notice and voila! After a few weeks of keeping my big mouth shut and working hard, I got offered the top job on the farm!

I now had my own little store room. I also used to accompany the head of the farm in his Land Rover. He was a nice man, typical tweed-and-green-wellies type. He also spoke very well, sort of posh and stately, like he was Lord of the Manor or top aristocracy. He seemed like gentry and had something almost regal about him. We got on and I got on with my borstal training.

I started getting into the weights and got really strong and fit. I started to get very muscular and this, coupled with my now quick-fire wit and confidence, meant I had all the respect I needed from my fellow inmates and the prison officers.

Lorraine, my girlfriend at the time, got arrested for the money she stole from the bank and got a non-custodial sentence. She used to visit and write regularly. I would (allegedly) get Lorraine to smuggle me some cannabis in there so I still managed to smoke it. I also became friends with a guy from Manchester – worldly wise, he became a tobacco baron! Sounds funny, hey, but he would lend a quarter ounce of tobacco for half an ounce back. A lot of the new guys did it from desperation or just to get in with the boys, I could see. I stopped smoking tobacco all together. I foolishly stored my friends' tobacco, money, etc. in my store room. Someone grassed us up, or we were just that blatant! Bye-bye good cushy job; hello block. I took the rap – well didn't say whose it was – I didn't know it was there. I got kept down the block. I did lots of reading and resting between meals.

I was allowed to go home for a week to help me prepare for the outside world. Whilst I was on home leave licence I was very careful to keep out of trouble. I went back to borstal for my last week, straight down the punishment block and I got a block discharge! I knew what I wanted: I wanted to be a successful criminal.

When I came out of borstal Lorraine had got a flat for us both to live in. The flat was down The Avenue area, which was private and a step up from the council estate. It was quite a posh area, not far from the local hospital and Lilford Woods and park.

So borstal came, and borstal went, after which from the age of twenty to twenty-eight I spent most of the time in and out of Strangeways. I'd accumulate a number of charges, eventually get no more bail, be placed on remand at Strangeways, then wait to get sentenced at the Crown Court. Once sentenced it would be back to Strangeways for allocation and then get sent to closed prisons because of my drug history. The closed & allocation Prisons I spent time in are Strangeways, Walton, Risley, Stafford, Brixton, Exeter Winston Green and Pentonville.

I enjoyed being welcomed out by my friends, well, associates. It wasn't long before I had my first fix again. I also found out that the associate who'd been supplying my girlfriend cannabis for me whilst in borstal, had also been supplying her with something else: sex! I was no angel myself. I remember sweet-talking a local model into sexual relations my first week out of borstal, and took her back to the flat that Lorraine had got for us. I was becoming more and more uncaring and unkind. I had become selfish, hard and lonely, hiding it all behind the front I had created, always joking, always making money, never satisfied unless out of my head on opiates. I was becoming a hardcore addict and very ill.

When I found out about Lorraine sleeping with this other guy, I went around to his flat one night. I felt betrayed by the two people closest to me, and I was angry. I banged on his door with a big knife in my hand. I kept banging, shouting his name. He either was not in, or wouldn't answer. Anyway, thank God he didn't because I'm sure I would have used the knife on him.

Here I was again, feeling betrayed, let down. I left Lorraine and went back home to mum. I began to drown my sorrows with Diconal, heroin, all the opiates I could get. Rather than buy the drugs off registered drug addicts who got prescriptions, I decided I wanted and needed to get a supply for myself.

I managed to get an appointment with a doctor who was prescribing these drugs to private patients. It was worth it because Diconal were worth about £4 each on the street. At first you got a really good hit, or rush, and then a buzz off two, but you could keep going every couple of hours. I got to see the doctor. I went with my mum and sister Pat to one of his surgeries in Lymm, Cheshire. This is a beautiful place that I'd been to years before as a boy, fishing at Lymm Dam. Here I was again, this time looking to get a script for a Class A controlled drug.

The doctor did an unusual thing and referred me back to my GP and recommended that I was prescribed methadone and cyclizine tablets. Methadone was becoming the conventional way to treat drug addicts now, as the police and doctors found out that addicts were injecting the Diconal tablets, which destroyed your veins and life very quickly. Before long, all your veins would collapse so people would inject into their femoral vein. The femoral vein is near your groin. You had to be careful not to inject into the arteries. This was the dangerous and desperate world I was now entering.

I saw my GP with the referral from the specialist and I was prescribed 8 x 10mg methadone a day and quite a few cyclizine. The cyclizine gave you the rush and were used as an anti-sickness drug. Although opiates make you feel so good and warm, sickness could be a side effect. Diconal were a mixture of dipipanone and cyclizine. Anyway, here I was now, getting a script at about twenty-one years of age. I would use more than my script soon and came up with all the excuses that addicts do – from going away on holiday, to putting them in the wash and losing them. It was a life now of getting high all the time. I wasn't going out socialising anymore; my only interest was the high and warm love I got from my drugs, legally!

Diconal was still the best though, so I started getting prescriptions off my doctor for other things and then writing Diconal on myself – 2 QDS. That was two, four times a day. I copied the doctors writing and Latin. I took them to the same chemist that I got my methadone from, so he didn't suspect. I had moved up from the days of forging sick notes for school. Now I was getting in a real state. To be honest, I really didn't care if I got caught or how many I took; I was in a right mess. My well-muscled and chiselled frame had become emaciated as I didn't eat much. What I did eat was all the wrong kinds of foods. You develop a sweet tooth as an addict, and I loved deserts and milkshakes!

An old associate from school, Keith Ashurst, had also got involved and addicted and we became close friends. His dad and grandfather had been world champion freshwater fishermen! Keith was in line to follow in their footsteps but was a huge disappointment. His dad owned maggot farms in England and Ireland so Keith used to deliver maggots to the fishing shops all over our area, I would go out with him. We were both high has kites. It wasn't long before I let him in on my secret of forging scripts, so we shared, forged, used together.

This went on for a while until eventually we became complacent, and went one step too far. The forgery wasn't that good – we got caught. We didn't really care. We were, after all, killing ourselves! We were looking death in the face every day. Every fix we took, every serious crime we committed, we were playing with death, prison, our lives, many times a day. Lonely, very ill and desperate.

CHAPTER 7

Near-Death Experiences

"Funny how a beautiful song could tell such a sad story"

SARAH DESSEN

D eath. I saw the face of death in my father when I was thirteen. My sister encouraged me to see him in his coffin as she felt it might be something I would regret later. He just had a plastic smile on his face and looked very unnatural. It was just a very spooky thing for a young guy to see in the coffin in the front room, with his white sort of robes on with the sacred heart of Jesus, a Roman Catholic icon, on the robe on his chest. I would rather remember the very much alive Dad, always smiling, always singing, always helping people and, yes, it was 'a life's work well done' as it says on the gravestone. I visited the grave recently with my brother John. I was able to tell him how I felt at the time and the way I went – not making excuses, but explaining how I felt. The day I stopped making excuses was the day my life started to change rapidly.

No more blame shifting, the past was in the past. I had been forgiven and the only person who could hold me back was me! How and where did this forgiveness come from, I was to learn not much later. This scripture is true:

> Praise the LORD, my soul;
> all my inmost being, praise his holy name.
> Praise the LORD, my soul,
> and forget not all his benefits –
> who forgives all your sins
> and heals all your diseases,

who redeems your life from the pit
and crowns you with love and compassion,
who satisfies your desires with good things
so that your youth is renewed like the eagle's.
(Psalm 103:1–5)

Please keep reading, you will see how scriptures like this can miraculously change even the most dire, desperate lives and situations.

I also saw my friend Keith Ashurst who later died of a drug overdose. After my conversion I saw him in hospital and I told his mum that God loved him and people loved him. She said people didn't love him. She meant people on the drug scene didn't love him. I went down to the psychiatric ward and saw the nurses and told them. They said that he was in good hands. It was just as though God was telling me Keith was in his hands, in good hands. Keith died later that night it was as if he had stayed awake for me, he'd sat at the end of his bed as if waiting to see me. It was very weird. People said dying people know that it's very weird about how they are expecting to see certain people.

Another guy I saw was Butch's brother, Kevin Jones. This was a guy who had done a lot of time in prison for murder or manslaughter. He came out and was very, very hooked on drugs and ended up committing suicide. Seeing him as well, just the face of death. I remember walking home with David Shovelton, the guy I had my Christian conversion with, and we were both very freaked out. He said, 'He didn't look very happy, did he, Terry?' and this made me burst out laughing hysterically because how can someone who is dead look happy anyway. I did see lots of death and I have had quite a few near-death experiences.

The first one was when I was about eighteen years of age, around the Punk scene time when I was very much into The Clash and Slaughter and The Dogs, a Manchester Punk band. I used to hang around Leigh, Atherton, Boothstown and surrounding areas of Leigh, all in Greater Manchester. Once we were all drinking and smoking weed in the King William pub at Boothstown, having travelled across the East Lancashire Road, the motorway that goes from Liverpool to Manchester. The guy driving the car decided to go through the light on red and as he went through he was hit, full impact, hard on, at about 70 mph at least! The car was sent into a series of spinning around whips. I curled up in a ball and thought I was ready to die.

The car span across the East Lancashire Road, went through a wall and ended up in somebody's front garden. We just got out of the car, dusted ourselves off and walked down to another pub on the other side of the East Lancashire Road, called the Greyhound. That was one near-death experience. And it was as matter a fact as that! We had no hope, so enjoyed ourselves as much as we thought possible. When you have nothing left to lose, you just don't care. Nobody loved me, I had nothing to lose. I have heard some of the recent rioters in the 2012 riots say the same thing. What's the answer? I believe we need a spiritual revival in the UK, just like in John and Charles Wesley's days, just like the Elim Pentecostal brothers Stephen and George Jeffries, just like *In Darkest England and the Way Out* by General William Booth. It's time for the church to really rise up and God is going to release the greatest evangelists this nation has ever seen. Ones who the world have completely written off, he is going to write them back on and use them for his glory, God knows we need it!

The next near-death experience was after one of our drug-taking binges. We were at my friend Tick's house. We'd eaten that night and had all been taking drugs all night. We woke up in the early hours of the morning and there was a blazing fire in the kitchen, an inferno. We all managed to get out. The house was filled with smoke, it was dark, it was thick but we managed to drag ourselves outside. And I remember I was pitch black except for just two lines down my cheeks where the tears had been rolling. We still managed to see a funny side and Tick said I looked like the skinny one out of Laurel and Hardy: 'That's another fine mess you've got me into, Stanley!'

That occasion was in my early to mid-twenties; another one was in my mid- to late twenties when I was with Paul Eckersley. I'd bought a car off Jake and Mark Winstanley who were two drug addicts on the scene. Mark introduced me to heroin. My first injection came about after a conversation with him when he was describing how good it was to sample the delights – or not delights – out of a dangerous-drug box from a chemist shop. I bumped into him and I got to sample these Class A drugs.

Anyway, I bought a car off his dad for fifty quid, an Avenger. I had prescriptions at the time. I was going around forging prescriptions and post office books – putting false entries into the post office books with blue carbon paper, putting money in the account and then once you'd drawn your first fifty quid out you had a legal stamp so you could keep drawing money out. I took fifty quid from each post office. I justified all this by saying that the post office and NHS could afford it. I saw myself as a kind of Robin Hood. (I was later to become a DJ under the pseudonym Robin Hoodz. This would be many years in the future. How did this happen? Stay tuned, it's an interesting and encouraging story. We'll get there soon. I'll stick to the interesting and exciting parts of my life story otherwise I'd need to do a series!)

I remember going on a cheque and prescription cashing spree in this car. Anyway, I got chased out of a chemist in Manchester somewhere – I think it was in Altringham or Sale. Anyway, Winstanley's parents got pulled in and arrested because they thought the dad had been taking the sons around cashing in prescriptions in the car, when it wasn't – it was me! Anyway I got caught for that later on.

Another night, in that same car, we'd been taking amphetamines and we got in into our heads to burgle a chemist. We ended up in a high speed chase which went on for miles and miles – I think it started in Wigan and ended up in Warrington. Cars were chasing us, wheels screeching. Paul Eckersley and Sean Parry were in the car with me that night. The police started ramming me. They came alongside in a Range Rover, and me, I was ramming them back! A policeman hung out the car and smashed my windscreen with his truncheon, which hit my nose and then knocked me off the road in a series of whips. I was ready to die, collapsed behind the wheel in the now crashed, stationary vehicle. I got rushed off to the police station and then hospital. Needless to say, I got charged with reckless driving. By the time the court case came up I was living in Newquay. I had to come back to answer to the charge.

Going back to when I was about sixteen years of age, I'd managed to persuade my mum to buy me a decent birthday present, my little Honda SS 50cc moped. Most of the Japanese had designed and produced these little dream machines! The Yamaha FS1E was the best, but I was really grateful for my Honda SS 50. I did all I knew to make it go faster. I filled the ports, something much more effective on a 2 stroke engine, but nevertheless it was the fastest Honda SS 50 in and around town. Boys will be boys. We used to go to drives to Rivington Pike which is a beautiful part of Lancashire with a big hill, castles, cafés, etc. It was a place where families went for days out and the motorbike gangs would congregate there too. Again this felt like a surrogate family. The older guys would always take great delight in saying how much they had paid for their bikes and how they had spruced them up. I was also spending time with my cousin Charles Bailey. He was having trouble with his separation and stuff and I was helping him decorate his first house. It was very, very cold and I had the stupid idea that if he turned the gas pipe on slightly and lit it, we would keep warm. Reluctantly he turned it on and off quickly. I lit it and a big ball of fire erupted through the whole kitchen! Again we were lucky to be alive.

After my borstal training, forging prescriptions, possession of drugs, the law finally caught up with me – I was heading back to Strangeways.

CHAPTER 8

HMP Prison

"Don't criticize what you can't understand."

BOB DYLAN

Eventually after the police and court process, the magistrates heard my case and I got six months in prison. Well I got nine months in total but three months was suspended. I was a big boy now, over twenty-one, so I went straight to the men's side of Strangeways. This time they inducted me just as before, but the doctor put me down the prison hospital wing B1. I was prescribed what they called a liquid cosh, largactyl, it was horrible. I felt like and walked like a zombie. I didn't sleep for weeks. This was what they called cold turkey. Your body stops making endorphins because the opiates replace them. Anyway, I felt, and was, really, really ill. They didn't taper you off back then in 1982. As Lennon sang, cold turkey, you got me, on the run!

I remember getting taken off the hospital landing, which was the bottom floor of B Wing, and I got put right up on B4. This was the top landing. You had to go on a long walk to the ground floor for your meals. It was on one of these trips that I suddenly had a fit. I got lock jaw – it was horrible, I couldn't speak. Would I be like this forever? The hospital officers came and gave me an injection and I started coming round to normal – phew, that was horrible. I ended up getting myself very fit and strong and finishing my sentence at Strangeways. I worked in a factory-like setting, putting electrical fittings together. I decided to settle for a life of 24-hours bang up in a cell, one hour for exercise, one shower a week, and as much gym as I could get. I also disciplined myself to regular press ups and reading. Again, just like at school, I devoured books and did have a little dabble in the Bible every now and again, but nothing serious. I got on well with fellow inmates and screws alike. I always had a laugh, told jokes and people kept telling me I was a top blag merchant, and I knew I was. This meant I had a silver tongue, a gift of the gab. Could I ever use my natural gifts for Good? Can you?

This sentence came and went and Lorraine and I tried to make a go of it again, but it was no good – the damage had been done; I didn't trust her again, which is choice I know, coming from the person I had sadly become.

CHAPTER 9

Her Majesty's Pleasure And Mine?

"You have every right to a beautiful life."

SELENA GOMEX

During the next eight years or so I spent most of my time in three places: on the street as we called it, on remand awaiting trial or sentence, or At Her Majesty's Pleasure doing a prison sentence! It seems funny, hey, that Her Majesty has her logo over my abode. I wonder if I would ever get to meet this lady, The Queen, whose residence I had now spent a bit of time in?

Everyone on the drug scene by now had started forging prescriptions, just copying what the doctor would write, but writing our own prescriptions. We had the intent of selling some, but we used most of them. I also became good with credit cards and post office books, sometimes making thousands of pounds a day, and in cash! I always bought the best clothes, but then would sell them, when desperate for a fix.

Again, I was back to Strangeways on remand for all sorts of charges – deception, drugs – and it was while on remand that I met one of the funniest, caring, crazy guys I would meet in my life: Segs Diamond. I was sat on my bunk and the door opened and this thick set guy came bouncing in.

'Allreet,' he said in his broad northern accent. 'I'm Segs Diamond.'

I introduced myself by saying, 'The infamous Segs Diamond'.

He told me later he thought I was taking the rise out of him calling him in famous, basically 'un famous' – not famous.

You see I'd heard of Segs years earlier when he was looking for one of my best friends Sean Parry. Sean had stolen a bottle of Diconal off one of Seg's dad's mates! You don't do that. I don't think Sean knew. Segs had pulled up in a car with a baseball bat looking for Sean. He said we could tell Sean that he was going to break his legs. I was with a friend of mine called Butch who had done borstal training with Segs. I later learned Segs had tracked Sean down and got some of the Dikes (Diconal) back. Sean was spared any pain as Segs' dad and Sean's had been big buddies. I think they had done borstal together.

I recounted this story to Segs and we had a good laugh about it. At that time half of Leigh was in Strangeways on remand, and half of Brixton. I knew all the Leigh guys, and Segs knew the Brixton guys so we were all introduced and got on great. All the Leigh guys were wrapped up in co-accused cases. This is where you are jointly charged for a crime. This would mean us going in a sweat box – it's like a horse box only you can just fit a human in, sat down! We would have banter all travelling to court and back weekly. We also spent time together on the exercise yard for an hour and we went to the gym quite often. I always went to the gym and built myself up.

Segs had boxing training and fought bare knuckle, so he began to try and teach me to box. He did this with the buckets we had in the cell. 'No, this is how you punch, put your shoulder behind it!' 'This is how you break jaws,' bam, 'This is how you knock people out! Come on.'

I was learning fast! I learnt how to knock people out with one punch. In the past I had relied on carrying weapons to defend myself but I wasn't the kind of guy who looked for violence. We would train a lot, read a lot, have the crack, telling stories of what we had been up to outside. Segs liked the way I impersonated people in my stories and got me to repeat them again and again. Of course prison was tough and boring but part of it was that we found the family we never had; we were close comrades. Yet when we were out of prison, because of the drugs, we would pull fast ones on each other.

Years later, after our prison sentences had sent us different ways, I had a weekend on the town with Segs. He was well respected and nobody messed with him. I was respected where I came from but Segs had a higher level violent touch. One day Segs pulled up at my mum's in a 7 series BMW with three other guys. Sean and I got in. My friend wanted me to get involved with them; Segs was a very well known and respected figure in the Underworld by now. I only found out months later that they were all carrying guns, a luger, a sawn-off shotgun and some other gun, and it was all very serious. Gang warfare was breaking out and it was all to do with controlling the doors – the bouncers who protected the pubs and clubs, the drugs that were being sold and all stuff like that. I was right in the middle of gang warfare. This was just before I was twenty-eight years of age and just before I was to have a powerful conversion. I think if I had not got converted, I would have been shot, or I would have shot somebody, or died of a drug overdose, or be doing life in prison. I could have easily become a murderer just like Moses or Saul of Tarsus, how did these guys start to change from heroes to well respected leaders and kings? What disciplines did they need or we need to live fruitful lives? Just like the Apostle Paul or King David disciplined themselves to give thanks to God daily – he's not insecure but God is a Mighty God and nothing is impossible with him – I have also disciplined myself to give thanks on purpose every day. There is a real power in it. God also inhabits the praise of his people. If you're ever down, the perfect answer is just keep praising God for who he is. Not just on Sundays or Wednesdays – try it every day!

> Rejoice always, pray continually, give thanks
> in all circumstances; for this is God's will for
> you in Christ Jesus.
> (1 Thessalonians 5:16–18)

Do you want to know God's will for your life? There you go, that's it!

I had soon accumulated a host of charges again and was back on remand, getting a fifteen-month prison sentence. Because of my drug and violent record I got sent to a Category B closed prison. This was hardcore; you had armed robbers, murderers (lifers) finishing off their sentences. This was Preston Prision in the north of the UK.

I got padded up with a guy from Manchester. We had heroin in common and got on well. I also had a neighbour called George. George was an interesting black guy. He walked with a kind of nobility and he had a good sense of humour. He dedicated his time to studying, reading and exercise. George was like an athlete. He used to motor around the exercise yard, squeezing every last drop of exercise out of it. He was in for three and a half years. He used to rob bank security vans singlehandedly! I found this fascinating, as he told his stories of wearing wolf man masks, screaming at the guard as he pounced from nowhere, grabbing the bag with £15,000 in. George also had nice clothes and a nice place to live, but again George loved smoking cocaine, rocks, crack! I have smoked it but it just made me sweat. I wanted more. Cocaine would soon go and you could spend a lot of money on it. George also had a flat in London next door to an apartment Jimmy Saville had! I was learning that with money you could get whatever you wanted. Everything, that is, apart from peace and eternal life.

That sentence soon came and went. I went home back to Greater Manchester and back to the drugs and my old cronies, as my mum would call them. I always determined I wouldn't, but did.

Next, I did a twenty-one-month sentence. How did I manage to get this? I'm glad you asked.

We travelled all around the country, Roy Pickering (my old school friend) and I, involved in crime, forging cheques and prescriptions. Roy was now a Hell's Angel type who had also got lost in the world of addiction. Paul Eckersley had also gone down this path. We were always involved in petty and not so petty crime. It was unorganised crime – we thought it was organised but we couldn't really organise the proverbial in a brewery. My exploits took me as far as the Balearic Islands with Sean Parry and a credit card I had obtained. Before we went there some friends and I allegedly broke into a chemist shop. I remember being on the Balearic Islands by a swimming pool with two beautiful ladies and my friend, all the money we wanted and all the drugs back home. That had been my dream all my life and I'd got it – yet I still felt very unhappy and empty. I was now in the position I had wanted to be in, yet I felt empty and bored. Yes having fun with sex, drugs, rock 'n' roll, the best hotel, beautiful ladies. It was a beautiful island, a beautiful place, but I wanted to go back to the UK to try and fill this gap with drugs. I still felt empty, a big aching hole on the inside.

As soon as we got back from holiday we even scored some heroin in Moss Side on the way back to get the drugs that we had – we were that addicted, in a bad way. We started to use all the drugs at our disposal. On one of the prescription forging-escapades going all around the country, we set off from Leigh and drove all the way down to the south coast of England. We were going to get as many drugs as we could and sell them. Like I say, it was organised crime, but on most of the jobs we got caught. More like disorganised crime!

I was with Roy Pickering in the Lake District when I started having a fit in the front seat of the car. When I came round I remember having a real sense of death, just the same sense of death I'd had when my dad died and I told Roy, 'I think my mum's died.'

'Terry, it's you what's died!' Roy said. My chest was hurting where he'd blown air into my lungs and brought me back round. My chest was all bruised and my lungs were very sore. All I can say is I felt a real bad feeling – I had been dead! Roy died about ten years ago now, from drugs. It's ironic that Roy Pickering, by the grace of God, had saved my life.

It was on one of these trips in the south of England with Roy that we got arrested. We got surrounded and taken into police custody. We were off our heads and got caught with all these drugs. They took us to the hospital. I remember coming round and seeing Roy running across the hospital ward with one of those paper gowns on with his bum sticking out at the back, which was quite a funny sight. We were in a right mess and got put in Exeter prison for a few weeks on remand. We had the crazy notion to stand up in the dock and represent ourselves and gave our tale of woe. Remarkably the court bailed us, much to the objections of the prosecution. It was remarkable, but that's the way we were. I remember reading a testimonial book about Christ whilst in Exeter prison, about a criminal called Fred Lemon who had had a Christian conversion. I really enjoyed it and I was praying there and then. I was asking God to help me, to come into my life, to help me at Court!

I had now probably done the equivalent in sentences and time on remand as the average life sentence but in instalments! Not clever, not good and it was getting boring now. I was institutionalised probably. Hard, lonely, living a life of deception to myself and others – would there be any way out?

CHAPTER 10

A Job And No Drugs!

"We're trying for something that's already found us"

JIM MORRISON

This time, upon release from prison, I was going to try and stop. I started going out for a drink and met some cool younger guys on the town, not villains or druggies! One of these was a guy called Jason Ramsden. Rammy was a nice guy – thickset, with designer-cut, bleached hair. We got on well together, shared the same taste in music and girls. We worked out at the gym together. He got me a job in sales. I sort of looked after Rammy as most guys were jealous of him – he had the looks, sports car and money. I was sort of his minder, nobody would mess with Rammy – he was Terry Eckersley's best friend. This was the hard guy who had been to prison, could handle himself and had had some very near-death experiences. And he didn't seem to care! But I also had a good sense of humour and caring side to me. I was known for being generous and I would look after people all the time; if they were getting bullied or needed a few quid for food, I would help people out.

Anyway, Jason Ramsden and I were good friends. We used to do the windows together. What I mean by that is we would be members of a canvass team, getting leads for the double glazing salesmen to follow up on. Jason had always wanted to go to Newquay, he'd been there on his holidays, a good surfing scene, a good holiday scene, so we went there one year. I left behind a girl who I'd been in a relationship with, but we'd been struggling; her mum didn't want the relationship to continue because of my reputation, although I was trying my best. Her name was Debbie and she worked in a travel agency, and in the middle of this relationship I went to Newquay. Debbie was a really attractive girl and a bit younger than me. I was staying clean with Debbie.

Anyway, back to Rammy and trying to keep my life on track.

His dad was a successful local business man, he had a gaming company. He supplied all the pool tables and gaming and invader machines. They were loaded! They had a big mansion with a swimming pool. I stayed there regularly; I was like part of the family. Rammy's dad even wanted to set us up in business with an arcade on the local estate. We were more interested in going out chasing girls! Michael Skeet also came out drinking with us. He was an old friend from St Mary's, my secondary school. Michael, like Rammy, was thickset and blonde, we were all working out and this showed in our physiques.

So Rammy and I went to Newquay which really was the English Riviera. I was clean while I was there, drug free, until I started to date a girl called Tarine. She was nineteen, blonde, beautiful, like a model. I met her on Fistral beach. She was younger than me; I was twenty-five by now. She was with her parents who didn't seem to mind the age difference because they could also see that she was in safe hands. What I mean by this is that they could tell I was caring and I could look after myself and others.

I got a job via the local job centre in Newquay. When I went to sign on for unemployment benefit they took my details and, sure enough, that week I had a phone call saying I had a job with a local building company. This was an excellent job. My first job was mowing lawns of a big estate of properties this building company had. I wore a pair of cut off jeans shorts, and just kept mowing away. It was similar to the window cleaning job and the window sales job – I was my own boss. I liked being my own boss; I didn't like people telling me what to do. This was the same with relationships – the first argument I had with my girlfriend I just broke up the relationship. Looking back I was very immature and wanted my own way the whole time. Yes, I was very immature and selfish.

So in Newquay, after the relationship failed, I persuaded a doctor to prescribe me opiates, blagged some drugs and started using again and was back into crime again – nothing heavy at first, just petty. I had to come back to Manchester for the court case I mentioned earlier – the time I had a high-speed car chase with the police and lost. This was a reckless driving case when we were under the influence of drugs and I just wouldn't stop for the police. The court case for this was later than I expected and the judge gave me prison. The authorities should have put this with lots of other charges I had at the previous court appearance, that way the charge and sentence would've more than likely run concurrent. I'd told my new girlfriend, a Scottish girl, I'd be back in five minutes! So here I was trying my best to go straight, moving away from Manchester, and this case should have been dealt with in my last prison sentence. But here I was again, back in prison. I got the worst judge on the Liverpool circuit who gave me a small sentence, less than a month. My barrister and I were dumbfounded; we couldn't believe I was going to prison. My barrister said he was going to put an appeal in for me. I wasn't that confident it would be any use, as I had been sentenced in the Crown Court. Back to the drawing board, here we go again. I was now being taken to Walton Prison in Liverpool. I was gutted. For once this just wasn't fair.

It was whilst I was in a prison cell at Walton Prison I read these famous words: 'If these walls were made of bread, I'd eat my way to Birkenhead' – typical Liverpool humour.

I had to laugh out loud; I was still much too hard to cry. I quote that every time I see a Scouser even to this day. Thank God for humour, it helped me get through some of those dark periods of my life. Two days later, though, my door opened. My barrister had been successful on appeal and got the sentence lifted. I was on my way back to Newquay, back to my new life and new girlfriend. But I was still under the heavy sentence of drugs and crime. Back in Newquay I got more and more involved in drugs. Even at this time I had a Christian landlady, I even met someone from the YMCA there. They all must have been praying for me, the hounds of heaven were on my tail. But my life was just a continuing spiral of sex, drugs and rock and roll – more drugs and rock and roll than sex, but there you go. After Newquay I went straight back to my old associates, and getting more and deeper into illegal activities, all drug based.

I had met other petty villains and drug dealers and users from all around the UK whilst in Newquay. I had now stopped hanging around with Rammy and Skeaty. I was back to my old ways. I ended up driving a brand new hire car which had been obtained by deception. I then decided to go and see a lady I had met who came from London and decided to take a trip back north to Manchester. Here I was, driving around in a brand new car with my life spiralling out of control with hard drugs and crime. My new life in Newquay hadn't worked. It wasn't just a case of getting away from where you live and all your known drug addict and crime associates – you see, I couldn't get away from myself! As I got physically weaker, again I would carry a big dagger or switchblade knife for protection.

So not long after coming home from Newquay I ended up getting a small, nine-month sentence and this is when I started seriously reading my Bible and it started impacting me. I was sent to Risley Remand Centre. I was to be working with an electrician fixing stuff around the prison. Risley was primarily a remand centre for prisoners awaiting trial. It had a bad reputation, Grisly Risley. I just took it in my stride. There were a couple of landings of convicted prisoners like me; I knew quite a few from former sentences. We got on well and we had good jobs, access to the gym – hey and a small sentence. I was very hardened by this time. I remember just standing up one day and punching a guy hard in the jaw and screaming at him to shut up! He did! He even apologised. This was after a session of him winding up some other prisoners and then me. This was a guy from a crime family in Manchester but I just didn't care anymore. However, greater forces were at work. I started to read my Bible, there's one in every cell. I picked it up and started to read Matthew, The Sermon on the Mount.

This guy made a lot of sense and I started sharing my thoughts with my friends as we queued for meals. I thought Matthew had it sussed, his take on life was, well, amazing! But it wasn't Matthew, it was the words of Jesus in Matthew. He was starting to speak to me! The words seemed to be jumping off the page.

> Therefore I tell you, do not worry about your life, what you will eat or drink; or about your body, what you will wear. Is not life more than food, and the body more than clothes? Look at the birds of the air; they do not sow or reap or store away in barns, and yet your heavenly Father feeds them. Are you not much more valuable than they? Can any one of you by worrying add a single hour to your life? And why do you worry about clothes? See how the flowers of the field grow. They do not labour or spin. Yet I tell you that not even Solomon in all his splendour was dressed like one of these.

If that is how God clothes the grass of the field, which is here today and tomorrow is thrown into the fire, will he not much more clothe you – you of little faith? So do not worry, saying, 'What shall we eat?' or 'What shall we drink?' or 'What shall we wear?' For the pagans run after all these things, and your heavenly Father knows that you need them. But seek first his kingdom and his righteousness, and all these things will be given to you as well. Therefore do not worry about tomorrow, for tomorrow will worry about itself. Each day has enough trouble of its own.

(Matthew 6:25–34)

Wow! These words had really spoken to my heart. I was starting to get excited about this person called Jesus.

Upon release and on my way home from prison, I stopped at Pat Parry's, Sean's mum, my friend who I had travelled the world and prison system with. I started to tell her about Jesus. I think she, like many others, would say, 'Terry Eckersley has finally lost it!' Pat Parry is a great lady. She did all she could to try and get her son Sean off drugs. This was from tying him to a chair, I heard, to lobbying to get drug services in Leigh, Greater Manchester. Pat did manage, along with another friend's mum, to get their children the drug services they were fighting for.

When I got out of prison I went to see my old friend David Shovelton and we started to study the Bible in a back room in a backstreet on the backside of Tyldesley, Greater Manchester. David was an old friend from the council estate I grew up on. I was now back living on the estate with my mum. We were all Punks together – David Shovelton, David Fairhust and Neil McCullough (my two old borstal friends). I had known David a long time, remember he was the guy who I was with when we both prayed a prayer and invited Jesus into our lives when we were twenty-one, about eight years before this meeting up. My life had come to a crossroads.

Herbie and I at the Sheffield YMCA. Great times there!

At the Sheffield YMCA with one of the heavy mob.

Terry and John preparing to see the Bee Gees at Wembley, 1997

First mission trip to Norway

CHAPTER 11

The Whole Room Lit Up

"You may say that I'm a dreamer
But I'm not the only one
I hope someday you'll join us
And the world will be as one"

JOHN LENNON,

IMAGINE

I gave my life to God when I was twenty-one. I did feel something but it wasn't earth shattering. It wasn't until I was twenty-eight that things really started to change. I had a hunger to read the Bible and learn more, so I went to David Shovelton's house. We decided we were going to study the Bible and seek God in the best way we could. This reminds me of the passage in the Bible where it says without faith it is impossible to please God and he is a rewarder of those that diligently seek him (Hebrews 11:6).

We settled down and started to read the passage in the Bible about the gifts of the Spirit in 1 Corinthians 12.

> Now about the gifts of the Spirit, brothers and sisters, I do not want you to be uninformed. You know that when you were pagans, somehow or other you were influenced and led astray to dumb idols. Therefore I want you to know that no one who is speaking by the Spirit of God says, 'Jesus be cursed,' and no one can say, 'Jesus is Lord,' except by the Holy Spirit.

There are different kinds of gifts, but the same Spirit distributes them. There are different kinds of service, but the same Lord. There are different kinds of working, but in all of them and in everyone it is the same God at work. Now to each one the manifestation of the Spirit is given for the common good. To one there is given through the Spirit a message of wisdom, to another a message of knowledge by means of the same Spirit, to another faith by the same Spirit, to another gifts of healing by that one Spirit, to another miraculous powers, to another prophecy, to another distinguishing between spirits, to another speaking in different kinds of tongues, and to still another the interpretation of tongues. All these are the work of one and the same Spirit, and he distributes them to each one, just as he determines.

Just as a body, though one, has many parts, but all its many parts form one body, so it is with Christ. For we were all baptised by one Spirit so as to form one body – whether Jews or Gentiles, slave or free – and we were all given the one Spirit to drink. And so the body is not made up of one part but of many. Now if the foot should say, 'Because I am not a hand, I do not belong to the body,' it would not for that reason stop being part of the body. And if the ear should say, 'Because I am not an eye, I do not belong to the body,' it would not for that reason stop being part of the body. If the whole body were an eye, where would the sense of hearing be? If the whole body were an ear, where would the sense of smell be?

But in fact God has placed the parts in the body, every one of them, just as he wanted them to be. If they were all one part, where would the body be? As it is, there are many parts, but one body. The eye cannot say to the hand, 'I don't need you!' And the head cannot say to the feet, 'I don't need you!' On the contrary, those parts of the body that seem to be weaker are indispensable, and the parts that we think are less honourable we treat with special honour. And the parts that are unpresentable are treated with special modesty, while our presentable parts need no special treatment. But God has put the body together, giving greater honour to the parts that lacked it, so that there should be no division in the body, but that its parts should have equal concern for each other. If one part suffers, every part suffers with it; if one part is honoured, every part rejoices with it.

Now you are the body of Christ, and each one of you is a part of it. And God has placed in the church first of all apostles, second prophets, third teachers, then miracles, then gifts of healing, of helping, of guidance, and of different kinds of tongues. Are all apostles? Are all prophets? Are all teachers? Do all work miracles? Do all have gifts of healing? Do all speak in tongues? Do all interpret? Now eagerly desire the greater gifts.

And yet I will show you the most excellent way.

(1 Corinthians 12:1–31)

The next night I was with David Shovelton again. We read chapter 12 the night before so it seemed sensible to read the next chapter 13.

> If I speak in the tongues of men or of angels, but do not have love, I am only a resounding gong or a clanging cymbal. If I have the gift of prophecy and can fathom all mysteries and all knowledge, and if I have a faith that can move mountains, but do not have love, I am nothing. If I give all I possess to the poor and give over my body to hardship that I may boast, but do not have love, I gain nothing.
>
> Love is patient, love is kind. It does not envy, it does not boast, it is not proud. It does not dishonour others, it is not self-seeking, it is not easily angered, it keeps no record of wrongs. Love does not delight in evil but rejoices with the truth. It always protects, always trusts, always hopes, always perseveres.
>
> Love never fails. But where there are prophecies, they will cease; where there are tongues, they will be stilled; where there is knowledge, it will pass away. For we know in part and we prophesy in part, but when completeness comes, what is in part disappears. When I was a child, I talked like a child, I thought like a child, I reasoned like a child. When I became a man, I put the ways of childhood behind me. For now we see only a reflection as in a mirror; then we shall see face to face. Now I know in part; then I shall know fully, even as I am fully known.
>
> And now these three remain: faith, hope and love. But the greatest of these is love.
> (1 Corinthians 13:1–13)

Now both chapter 12 and 13 had spoken about gifts and miracles and faith and this gift of tongues, a heavenly language that God gives as a gift to his followers. I asked David, 'What is this tongues that keeps getting mentioned?' At this question my friend could speak in tongues and he did, there and then. We prayed and I received the gift of interpretation – I could understand and communicate what God was saying through the heavenly language.

When my friend was speaking in tongues, I felt the Holy Spirit telling me that Jesus died so my sins could be forgiven. I broke down and cried but the whole room lit up! It was amazing. The same power displayed at Pentecost saved me! I felt clean, loved; I wept like a baby and felt brand new (2 Corinthians 5:17).

David had never seen me cry before and he was really shocked. He kept on asking me, 'What's up, Terry, are you OK? What's wrong? Why are you crying?'

I repeated over and over again 'Jesus has died for me, Jesus has died for me.' I had heard this many times before, I had seen this on posters, read it in books, but this time it made sense. It was as if someone who really loved me, like my mum, had jumped under a bus and died so that I could be forgiven for all the wrong I had done in my life! Also, in addition to feeling forgiven, all the years of loneliness and being hard just seemed to melt away. I felt loved and comforted – wow! This was amazing, God really loved me.

> Therefore, if anyone is in Christ, the new creation
> has come: the old has gone, the new is here!
> (2 Corinthians 5:17)

I remember cycling home from David's. I went there as a drug addict and criminal. I had started to get violent just before then. I was taking steroids along with all the other drugs so I was at my worst. Whenever the police came to arrest me they would send lots of police in cars and vans. I was a handful. Now I was cycling home feeling like a new person, all clean on the inside. My spirit was singing 'Onward Christian Soldiers', the old Salvation Army hymn.

So here I was now at this crossroads: I couldn't go the way of drugs and crime anymore, but this was the life I had lived and I didn't know how to go the other way. I had been living this life for many years now and didn't have any help, anybody who believed in me. I didn't know how to change.

I had nothing to do so I just stayed in and spent valuable time with my mum. Everyone seemed to have written me off but I was being genuine, for once in my life. I felt like the boy who cried wolf. Now I was being sincere nobody believed me!

However, I still had outstanding charges relating to drugs and crime. I went to court and, bam, I got a twenty-one-month prison sentence. I had genuinely been wanting to get into a rehab now, I couldn't live a life of drugs and crime anymore. I spent the first part of my sentence in police cells. We kept getting moved around from police station to police station. This was because there had been a riot in Strangeways. My friend Sean had been in there at the time, he said it was crazy. An inmate had grabbed the microphone off the prison chaplain and enticed everyone to riot. Prison officers were overpowered and prisoners got keys and went rioting through the prison, stealing all the drugs from the hospital wing and looting and rioting. This went on for weeks, and made national and international news. Because Strangeways was out of action, we spent the first part of our sentence in police cells up and down the country.

Because of my now violent and hard drug record, I was allocated to go to a closed prison in Stafford. I had been to Stafford years before as a Bowie fan. I bought tickets when I had my first job and saw him at Bingley Hall Stafford. That trip and gig was amazing. Now I was going to what was meant to be one of the toughest prisons in the UK. I was used to this by now, as I'm sure you can understand, only this time it was different, this time I was a changed man.

I quickly got into a routine there, working out in the gym. In some ways I started to enjoy myself there – again very, very weird but I just felt I fitted in there OK. I had a picture up in my cell called 'Christ is Risen', and I was regularly reading my Bible and I was now a Christian. I understood nothing but knew Jesus had died for me.

Anyway I remember starting performing on the wing, that is just being outgoing and expressive. The authorities saw that as rebellion and I got put down on the block on good order and discipline – really taken out of the main population of the prison because they felt that I could cause disputes, fights or trouble in the prison. And it was when I was down the block that I started reading my Bible again and something spoke to me whilst reading the Psalms of David. There is so much wisdom in Psalms, and I realised that I had a lot to be thankful for and that I should stop being a fool. Things were a lot better with the general prison population – gym, friends, more socialising and freedom. We had shared exercise for an hour a day and we also had some association time which was playing table tennis, darts, watching television. I'm told now that prisoners have televisions and DVDs and computer games in their cells. We could only have radio and cassette tapes! CDs and DVDs hadn't been invented or come on the market then! Anyway, like the lesson I learned way back in borstal, I lost the chip off my shoulder. I stopped trying to be smart and rebellious. This change in my heart and behaviour was soon noted and I was allowed back up on the wing.

I was welcomed back as I had made lots of great friends. I seemed to have this unusual ability that I was able to connect with everyone, and I did have this unusual positivity about me. I now know this to be the gifting, anointing and favour of God! Wow! Let's not rush on, just pause there. God, who made heaven, earth, you, me, everything and everyone, and he so loved the world he sent his son Jesus to die for us! This is the whole truth of the gospel, and can only bring an attitude of gratitude to any person in any circumstance when believed and received.

I had been going to church in prison and I had been sharing my faith in a very natural and friendly way, I hadn't been taught by anyone yet. It was a national prisoners' week and I was handpicked, remarkably, to go out on this walk around the country to highlight prisoners' week. We went to different cathedrals to be blessed by different bishops and to stay at different churches.

This was amazing seeing as that not long before I had been down the punishment block. A group of us, who were now deemed low risk, were picked and we started to train for this huge event. There were about five of us, all different characters, different colours, shapes and sizes. I got on well with an older black guy called Mighty. He was from the ghetto, yet he carried himself well, a little grey hair at the sides of his well groomed short hair, and neat and classy prison uniform, and gold teeth. He was amusing and intelligent and was a genuine guy. The other four of us were white guys. We had two prison staff with us, one was the prison chef, who was also a prison officer, I think of PO level – that's a senior post. (There are officers, senior officers, principal officers and then assistant governors and then a governor.) Bill the Chef, his name was, had had a very powerful Christian conversion along with his wife and some other close friends. Bill was an evangelist; he told everybody about Jesus, and he radiated with the love of God. The other senior officer who was with us was also a gym officer. He was not a Christian but he was a nice guy. We were an interesting bunch of people, all excited about this great opportunity to get out of normal prison life. A great adventure.

We did a very long walk around the country, as I said, to highlight prisoners' week. We slept in churches and other accommodation along the way. The churches were all really nice to us, we got fed well and we were prayed for everywhere we went. I still had my personal faith experience, was seeking God in my own way. Some of the people, including Bill, seemed too full-on for me, holding their hands in the air in worship, you have to do this and not do that. I listened but also was going to work this out on my own – and I would advise you to do the same. The apostle Paul also encourages us in his letters to do the same, so that our faith rests on the power of God and not on the teachings of man. This kind of faith is unshakeable when tested to the utmost of testing, I'll share some of that later. But for now I have learned that faith comes in three different ways:

'Faith comes by hearing and hearing the word of God' (Romans 10:17), so the more we hear and read the word of God faith comes. That's why it's good practice and a good discipline to keep getting or feeding yourself the word of God, especially when we are facing challenges. Find the relevant Bible passages to build your faith and get victory in the battles we are fighting. I have personally now developed this discipline into my life. Also the discipline that we then get in our lives qualifies us as a disciple of Christ, a disciplined one. I have had lots of battles as you now know with drug addiction, lust, needing provision. I have learned what the Bible says about these challenges and I have then applied these scriptures, believed them, prayed them, declared them and God has never let me down. He never will. Even when we are unfaithful, he is still faithful; he cannot deny himself! That, too, is a Bible promise!

The second way we get faith is it is a gift. We read in the Bible that all believers have been given a measure of faith; some believers have been given what's called a gift of faith. This gift of faith, along with the other gifts of the Holy

Spirit, is talked about in 1 Corinthians 12. I have been given this gift of faith quite a few times for different situations. I knew by a gift of faith I would have a wife, though I waited about fifteen years for this to come to pass! If you're waiting, praying, believing God for a partner, don't be discouraged. I've known people not wait half this time: some hardly wait whilst others are still waiting! I have also learned that we need to give God something to work with, so coffees and dinner dates with potential partners is a must. I'll tell you more of my own story later.

I have also had to have faith for my first job at the YMCA. I was prayed for at church for a job. When I was prayed for a great peace came over me and I wept tears of joy. I knew by the gift of faith a job was on the way. I later got the job at Sheffield YMCA. Again, it was wise and practical to be studying and doing voluntary work. I was giving God something to work with. I had been volunteering at church, the YMCA, another Christian charity, the European tennis championships and the European swimming championships. In later years I have been given a gift of faith for many different situations, people and things. Again, stay tuned and I'll share them in detail later.

The third way we get faith is by a fruit of the Holy Spirit. This is spoken of by the apostle Paul in Galatians 5. What I love about this part of the book of Galatians is that it speaks about the sinful nature, then the fruit of the Spirit. The fruit of the spirit grows as we grow as a Christian, like real fruit grows. Slowly, seasonally, planted in good soil (find a good church and stay planted there) and fed well. This will come from the different pastors, teachers and evangelists you hear in church, but also feed yourself. We can now all see and listen to either the Bible or many great ministers on our phones! Another thing with fruit is that it is only cultivated in challenging situations. How have I got the fruit of patience in my life? By having to wait. How do we get the fruit of faith? By continuing our walk of faith. It will suddenly dawn on you – wow, I have got faith for this or that. What I love about walking by faith is that we can help so many other people. In our church services when we would be praying for jobs for people, I would be praying to be able to employ many people. I've just moved on from something I started from scratch by faith – the gift and fruit – to employing over 200 staff! I'll share that full story later, it's a good one. By faith they always are!

Right, back to the walk around England to highlight prisoners' week…

After this amazing experience I went back to prison waiting to be released. Upon my release I went back to Leigh in Manchester, and spent a lot of time at home with my mum. This was a precious time and she could see that I had changed. We got on well and she was no longer worried about me every time I went out the door, wondering if she would see her son alive again. I was very much changed. I didn't want to go the wrong way but didn't know how to go the right way. I applied to go into a drug rehabilitation centre and got a place in Phoenix House in Sheffield, but I still had an outstanding charge of trying to escape from custody. This was from when I was being held in the police cells when Strangeways was closed because of the riots. I had this silly notion that I should try to escape. I had a good go, but I didn't even get out of the court building. I was in the dock in court listening to the proceedings when out of the blue, unexpected, in this quiet, austere atmosphere, I placed one hand on the dock rail and skilfully leapt over it! The policeman followed me. I headed for the court doors, my heart beating faster and faster, adrenaline was racing through my veins like a racing car. It was like it was all in slow motion as I was moving; all eyes on me as I somehow sprang like a gazelle in my training shoes. It wasn't any good. Bam! I was rugby tackled by one policeman, strangled around the neck by another, then it was scrum down and I was the ball.

I went to Bolton Crown Court; it wasn't to be another custodial sentence, not prison, so I was able then to make a decision and was sentenced to go to Phoenix House Rehabilitation Centre in Sheffield. To be honest, I was tired of this life of drugs now. Although I was a Christian I didn't have the faith or power to get off drugs, yet. I also didn't know how to live a normal life. I had become self sufficient. I'd looked after myself from the age of thirteen, when my dad had died. It was even before then, looking back, that I had felt like an orphan. I had to cook for myself, protect myself. But from an innocent child who had been abused in many different ways with hardly any love shown to him, here I was, a hardened drug addict and criminal, now violent. I was lonely, scared and depressed. I had been converted to Jesus, my heart had been touched and the healing had started but I knew I needed a lot more help, more love, more compassion to start this new life.

But the temptation, the battle was so strong. I'd met some ladies who had money and a lot of drugs. They asked if I would go with them, now, as we could have one last good time. The battle was raging within me, my bag was packed. I could have one last good time with these friendly ladies, who had lots of drugs with them – and their good looks. I felt tortured, sweat appearing on my forehead as ten seconds went by – it was like ten minutes.

'Are you coming then?' one of the sexy girls said with a glint her eye.

My heart was pounding by now, ddum, ddum, ddum. 'No,' unexpectedly came from my mouth, 'I need to get the train to Sheffield.'

I felt good inside. This was perhaps the smartest decision I had made in twenty-seven years! My new life was about to start as I was leaving the old Terry Eckersley behind. He was now dead and buried; the new creation in Christ was interested, and now slightly excited about what the future may hold.

I managed to get on the train – I say managed because the temptation was so strong but somehow I was able to resist and get to Sheffield. When I got to Phoenix House, I told the guy I just wanted to be open and sincere. When he asked if I had taken any drugs, I told him that I had smoked cannabis and so I had to go and stay in the Salvation Army hostel that night, in Sheffield. Whilst staying this one night in the Salvation Army hostel, a soup kitchen came around. This was being provided by local Christians. I got some soup and was chatting and one of the Christians said that God an amazing plan for my life. Could he? Really?

But the next day I was taken in at Phoenix House: 'We shall rise from the ashes of our defeat. We are here because we have no refuge from ourselves.' This was part of the Phoenix philosophy that I was going to learn over the next few months.

It was an interesting group of people in Phoenix House, of course all ex-addicts, prostitutes from Manchester. There was a mixed-race lady who was really attractive and made it known she was attracted to me. We got on well and recounted the various villains and druggies we mutually knew in Manchester. She was from Moss Side, the notorious part of Manchester that was being called Gunchester and Madchester in the press and media. I also met a guy from Glasgow; he was very angry and had sold himself as a rent boy to raise money for drugs. We got on well together and had similar tastes in music. He was very serious about the Phoenix philosophy and was determined to get through it and kick the habit that had taken him to such low situations. How do you separate low? An addict will do crazy and degrading things to get drugs but always has a way of justifying it, and there is always someone who is more degrading than them, so they can quote this and justify it! Everyone from drug addicts to prostitutes – I don't go that far, I'm not as bad as this kind or that kind or suchabody is there cry of justification.

Phoenix House was full of about twenty people and types from all over England really; they'd been hardcore addicts who wanted to get free from this. A lot of the help offered at Phoenix was based on the feeling approach: how does that make you feel? How does that really make you feel? If you got angry you had to write it down and put it in a box, and once a week there would be confrontation groups. The whole issue of the confrontation was getting behind the real anger that caused you to feel that way at the time; and many people would sit and relate tales of relationship issues, childhood abuse, all stuff like that. You would be doing very well in there if you did open up and share a lot – according to the Phoenix philosophy.

I sort of enjoyed it there really: the food was great, the community was great, there were a lot of people who had gone through the programme and were free from drugs. Of course this was very admirable and brought hope. They worked there and not just as support staff, but as the director and some managers. I tried my best there and I really enjoyed being honest in groups, in the mutually supportive environment.

I ended up on a contract where you would just clean the kitchen or you would go around with a bucket and just doing cleaning duties. No-one could speak to you, or you couldn't speak to anyone: it was all so you could get more in touch with your feelings. I did explore a lot; you went back through your past, through your childhood, you wrote it all down, you shared on it. But for me there was lots of stuff – lots and lots of stuff – and it never brought any resolution, and so I got very disillusioned with the Phoenix approach and environment.

CHAPTER 12

Church, Celebrities, Gangsters And The YMCA

"I get by with a little help from my friends."

JOHN LENNON

I left Phoenix House and went to the local DHSS. I had given my all to the programme. It had done its best in living in a therapeutic environment. Yes, it was a beautiful mansion in the better side of the city in Sheffield. Yes, there were some great interesting recovering and recovered addicts. There were also some excellent professionals. But, in short, I was disillusioned with the heart of the programme. So, after much wrestling with myself, my peers and the staff – not WWF but internal wrestling – I made the decision to leave. My friends and the staff tried to persuade me to stay. Yes, it was sudden, yes it was unplanned, yes it was silly, but I had made up my mind. I walked down the lonely road of Phoenix House with most of my possessions in a bin liner.

I went to the homeless section at Sheffield City Council and because I was a priority need after being classed as and given disability benefit, I was soon processed and ended up in a bed and breakfast – very nicely furnished, clean, brand new and with a cooked breakfast every morning!

This seemed quite good for the moment, but what about my future? So, here I was in a bed and breakfast, I was homeless and vulnerable in a strange city. It reminds me of The Jam song 'Strange Town' written by Paul Weller. One of the lines includes buying an A to Z guidebook and a list of YMCAs! Paul Weller, the YMCA and me? Was there any significance in this? It will all make perfect sense... later!

It was while on the walk around the whole of the UK to highlight prisoners' week that we all opened up more to the Christian faith, people praying for us and bishops blessing us. We went to Sheffield an were going to stay at the YMCA but they had to change that location and we stayed at the Kings Centre Church instead. Sheffield YMCA was in Broomhall and it was felt that this area, where there were many prostitutes and drug addicts, would place us in a situation where drugs were readily available. I wondered then if I'd ever get to see Sheffield YMCA. Would I ever end up in Broomhall? I didn't on that trip. Would anything in my past, in my future, in my destiny allow me to go into the streets of Sheffield to meet some of these prostitutes and drug addicts and maybe be a positive influence? Not on that trip. The trip went very, very well; York Minster was used for the final celebration and we had a really good time.

Anyway, here I was in Sheffield again. And some Christians started to reach out to me. While I had been in Phoenix House, I had always gone to church and took lots of people with me. I still had the deep faith that I had from my experience with David Shovelton when I realised Jesus had died for me! This faith was locked in my bones, just like Jeremiah of old.

I now started to go to a local church with these new Christian friends of mine. They all had amazing conversion experiences: one was an ex-druggie and ex-prostitute, one was an ex druggie and music business exec, she had also been caught up in sadomasochism which had led to her having to have EST (electric shock treatment) and medication. Eventually she lost all hope and took a large overdose. Her brother had married a Christian lady and they all prayed for her and miraculously she came around after a coma everyone medical had said she wouldn't come out of. This was a few years before I met her. Her name was Sarah. She helped me get a room to rent off a lady in the church near Broomhall Park Sheffield. I was indeed blessed. I was sensing God's presence in the worship, and scriptures would jump out at me! Faith comes by hearing and hearing the word of God (Romans 10:17). I was learning fast. God loved me personally and had a plan for my life. I could speak to him direct and hear from him direct through his word – the Bible. I started doing community courses, qualifications and then I saw God was a provider so I started to believe and pray for a job.

Because of the anger issues and jealousy, which I believe are closely linked, I had a big argument with Sarah. This led me to smashing a wardrobe up with my bear hands and feet. I had a supernatural evil power when resorting to violence or intimidation or when people lied to me, which is what Sarah was doing to me at the time. This betrayal I felt made me very, very angry.

I immediately repented, said I was sorry to God and felt really, really remorseful. I went to my Bible and again the words jumped off the page!

> Is anyone among you in trouble? Let them pray.
> Is anyone happy? Let them sing songs of praise.
> Is anyone among you ill? Let them call the elders of the church to pray over them and anoint them with oil in the name of the Lord. And the prayer offered in faith will make the sick person well; the Lord will raise them up. If they have sinned, they will be forgiven. Therefore confess your sins to each other and pray for each other so that you may be healed. The prayer of a righteous person is powerful and effective.
> (James 5:13–16)

I rang the pastor up immediately, and wanted to confess

some sin, not anybody else's, I often joke, I wanted to confess my sin. He said he would pray for me and wait until church the next morning. I did attend that next morning and the son of one of my new mums in the faith was preaching.

He was called Hughes Redhead and his mum Claire was a beautiful woman; she was a stereotypical Pentecostal black lady. She had brought up nine children by God's grace, her motherly love and deep devotion to God and help from him.

Claire deserves a whole book dedicating to her, a few chapters are not enough, but I will do my best. This lady was, and is, the closest I had seen and met to Jesus! This is very interesting if you have read the multi-tens-of-millions best-selling book, the Bible. And so is the best selling book "The Shack". It's worth a read. The interview my friend J.John did with the author is one of the best I've seen! And I've seen many interviews – people and their stories fascinate me.

Right, back to Claire. When she prayed things happened. She would pray the word of God, pieces of scripture verses, sing them and pray them. She would operate in the gifts of the Spirit mentioned in 1 Corinthians 12 and seen in the New Testament from the disciples being baptised in the Holy Spirit at Pentecost, a new power and boldness came upon them. Peter the disciple running scared, denying Jesus, became the rock on which God would build his church.

Claire had a prayer meeting every Tuesday and I would attend. The hospitality she shared with anybody was amazing. She always had a large selection of goodies from home-made Jamaican cake and biscuits to tea, coffee, cold drinks. As I said, though this was exceptional hospitality it was a wonderful aperitif to the main course! Claire would start to pray, declaring God's faithfulness, his grace, his power; she would start to pray in tongues, she would get interpretations – God Almighty would speak to us and comfort us. Wow! These were very special, very sacred moments from a lady who opened her heart, her life, everything, to the main love in her life, Jesus. I became a friend to the family at first, getting to know all the family. Claire called me her adopted son and never forgot my birthday. I was blessed with a surrogate spiritual mother and she also mothered me naturally speaking to. I and many others owe Claire and the God she serves our lives, because without Claire and many others in the church, without Jesus and his church, I would not be alive!

Back to the story... Claire's son Hughes was an evangelist and assistant pastor in the church I went to, Hope City Church, then called The Hope of Sheffield Christian Church – quite a mouthful hence the name change. Hughes was a God-called Evangelist (please see Ephesians 4 which explains the gifts the risen Christ gave to the body of Christ, the church). The evangelist proclaims good news, the gospel, encourages others into maturity in Christ and prays for the sick and sometimes the sick get healed. Why do some get healed and others not? I don't fully understand, but God is a healer; I've found this out in my life and in the lives of others that I have prayed for all around the world. What if they don't get healed? What if they do?

Sunday morning, I'm sat at the back of the church. Worship started, I felt the presence of God, God lives in the praises of his people. Do you need a touch from God? Start to worship him. We went through the formalities of a church service: offering, notices and then the moment I had been waiting for with great expectancy, the preacher Hughes was introduced. He said he was preparing something else when the Lord had directed him to preach a sermon he had preached before! I was encouraged, sat on the back row feeling closer now after feeling a million miles away from God.

The preacher started telling the story of blind Bartimaeus in Mark 10:46–52:

Then they came to Jericho. As Jesus and his disciples, together with a large crowd, were leaving the city, a blind man, Bartimaeus (which means 'son of Timaeus'), was sitting by the roadside begging. When he heard that it was Jesus of Nazareth, he began to shout, 'Jesus, Son of David, have mercy on me!'

Many rebuked him and told him to be quiet, but he shouted all the more, 'Son of David, have mercy on me!'

Jesus stopped and said, 'Call him.'

So they called to the blind man, 'Cheer up! On your feet! He's calling you.' Throwing his cloak aside, he jumped to his feet and came to Jesus.

'What do you want me to do for you?' Jesus asked him.

The blind man said, 'Rabbi, I want to see.'

'Go,' said Jesus, 'your faith has healed you.' Immediately he received his sight and followed Jesus along the road.

The preacher talked and preached very powerfully about Jesus being the same yesterday, today and forever (Hebrews 13:8), he shared about the disciples, his minders, trying to hush Bartimaeus, keeping him away from Jesus. He said he felt that there was someone in the congregation who felt like people – disciples – had been pushing them away, just like Bartimaeus of old. He was right; it was me! So I responded when the call was given that anybody who wanted to be healed should come to the front of the church. I came up to the front to be healed. Another member of the prayer team prayed for me but nothing happened. I stayed at the altar, then the man of God came over. When he laid his hands on me and prayed in tongues he said let all mental scars be healed in the name of Jesus. It happened again: I fell to the floor crying! Weeping under the healing power and love of God! Wow! I was healed! Forever! It was like electricity and then liquid love being poured into and all over me. The power and the love of God were coursing through my body, mind and spirit. I could have stayed there all day, and one day I will! Will you join me? Or will you not spend eternity in the love and presence of God. There are streets of gold and everybody's welcome! The ticket's free, the invite is now; it's a free gift to us, but it cost a perfect and righteous judge as well as a loving father everything. It cost God the very life of his son. His crucifixion paid the price for the sin of the world; the divine exchange.

This healing now brought me perfect peace. I had never had this before; I had always been restless, now everything had changed. I used to go for walks around Endcliffe Park in Sheffield. The park was two minutes away from where I lived and had a flowing stream, woodland, a big playing field, ducks and a café. We used to go there from Phoenix House, the rehab. It all looked different now – I was overwhelmed with the beauty of nature, God's creation. I was free, at peace. That's what saved means I've since learned, not just saved from ours sin, but nothing missing nothing broken, complete, whole; for the first time in my life I felt and was whole!

Things were moving on, and things were developing. The voluntary work was going great. I was training at the gym at Sheffield YMCA where I had a free membership because my voluntary work was putting out and helping to set up a gymnastic club in the multi-purpose sports hall they had. I did this every Saturday and consequently got to know all the staff at the YMCA and felt part of the team. I also did a fitness instructors course and became qualified in fitness instruction. I volunteered at the European tennis and swimming championships, both held in Sheffield, two successive years. Sheffield was becoming known as the city for sport. I did a community development course – I was really making up for the years I didn't apply myself at school. We were being taught as a church about having an excellent spirit and work ethic. A spirit of excellence in all we do and say, going the extra mile. I am eternally grateful for the ministry of Dave Gilpin and Hope City Church; once again, without him and his ministry I would not be alive today.

So here I was now in Sheffield, really enjoying my new life. I was free from drugs and crime. I was in a local church that was doing a great work and had an amazing community of families and believers. During one of the services, in a time of ministry and prayer, Pastor Dave asked for people who needed a job to raise their hands. I did and a group of people then surrounded me and everyone started to pray for people in the church. Again I felt the power and love of God – this is how God lets me know things have happened. I knew by faith that I had a job – I just needed to practically process this.

God then provided a great job for me at the YMCA, where I went on to become CEO, I got this little flat, this beautiful flat with this beautiful panoramic view; but below me I had a very interesting character called Deke Rivers, Deke Rivers was a character in an Elvis Presley film. But Deke Rivers didn't just think he was Elvis in a film, Deke Rivers thought he was Elvis all day long, but he was very small, he had the quiff, but he played Meatloaf All the time. That's alright if you're hearing it once or twice, but I was hearing it one, two, three, four, five o'clock in the morning and I had just got my new job. He wasn't playing Graham Kendrick, Matt Redman or Hillsong Darlene Zschech, all Christian worship leaders, he was playing 'Bat out of Hell' and he was sending me crazy!

I put as many tracts under his door as I could, I tried telling him of my new found faith when I could get near him, then mail started to get stolen, this was a heat of the moment experience for Terry Eckersley... the crunch came, I met him head on in the corridor and I started confronting him about the 'Bat out of Hell' which I was getting concerned about and about stealing mail, especially my birthday card from America which would have had dollars in, a very important issue.

He pulled one of those faces at me, and started squaring up at me; in the heat of the moment I chased him all around that block of flats, I chased him straight up to his door and he ran behind his door and hid there. He said you blankety blank, blank, blank, Christian; I said you said you blankety blank... no I didn't...! I said you'd better thank God I'm a Christian or this door would be coming in Deke Rivers! I said it in the heat of the moment, man does his worse, when? In the heat of the moment... are you getting it? I went back to my room, lay down on my bed, picked up my bible and I said I'm sorry Lord; and I opened it and read Luke 6. Luke 6:27-28 (The Message)

> "To you who are ready for the truth, I say this:
> Love your enemies. Let them bring out the best
> in you, not the worst. When someone gives you
> a hard time, respond with the energies of prayer
> for that person. If someone slaps you in the
> face, stand there and take it. If someone grabs
> your shirt, gift-wrap your best coat and make a
> present of it. If someone takes unfair advantage
> of you, use the occasion to practice the servant
> life. No more tit-for-tat stuff. Live generously".

And exactly the same scripture that I read then, and God spoke to me very powerfully, I saw it again when I saw Mel Gibson's film 'The Passion of the Christ' forgive them for they know not what they do, comes from the mouth of Christ and His faithful disciples.

These words jumped of the page, especially, "I will show you the man". I sensed that if I prayed for and blessed my enemies and those that cursed me, God would reward me. And use me, for His glory. This discipline was to put me in good stead for my vocational calling.

Just before I was to get any job – just tracking back a little – a board member at the YMCA, a guy called Charlie Shuttleworth (a very rich business man, who'd started the Western Jean Company who'd become a Christian) had set up a wine bar in the city and brought in Herbie Armstrong to run it for him. Herbie had an interesting career path. A slim, tall, charismatic guy from Belfast, he had done everything from running a hot dog stall to getting the legendary Van Morrison his first singing gig! This led to Herbie touring and playing on all the early Van Morrison albums. He played rhythm guitar on such classics as 'Bright Side of the Road' and the iconic album, Into the Music. I have a signed copy of this multi-platinum selling album.

I went to meet Herbie; he was stood against the bar of The Slug and Fiddle. He welcomed me in his warm Irish accent and charming way. I liked this ultra cool guy – he had some amazing accomplishments under his belt, yet he was warm, friendly, caring and genuine. I didn't know it then but Herbie was to become a lifelong friend, along with his ex-model wife Lisa and their kids,

Anyway, I sat down with Herbie over my diet coke.

He shared the whole story of how he had met Charlie on holiday. Charlie was an enthusiastic Christian and a big Van Morrison fan. I don't know if you have noticed but because of Van Morrison's mystical music and spiritual lyrics, Vans fans are more than fans; they become part of his almost cult following. His music is amazing. He's written some great songs. There's also this element of mystery about him. Herbie, in-between telling me interesting and colourful stories of the celebrities he's met at various after-show parties

– Robert De Niro, Johnny Depp, anyone you can think of – told me of meeting Charlie and Jackie Shuttleworth on the Algarve and how Charlie had asked Herbie to head this classy music wine bar that served great food. He had kitted the place out with original floorboards, lots of old pine tables and chairs, The Slug and Fiddle was a very special place.

They were about to open soon and they needed a head bouncer, a doorman, and did I know any Christian doormen? He was asking me to be a Christian doorman? There you go – an oxymoron, a contradiction in terms. But I went to see Charlie and the other directors. I'd met Herbie and clicked with him immediately and I was accepted for the job. It all seemed very seductive and cool and celebrity. But just before I got the job, it just didn't feel right; it didn't feel a good environment to go back into at that time of my life and I felt I had to say no. So I went there and said, 'I'm really sorry, it doesn't feel right, but God bless you and I hope everything goes OK.' Going back home that evening I just felt the real presence of God in my life because God was going to honour me for putting him first. And this came with the YMCA job.

Jesus had saved me of my sin, he healed me, provided for me, and then I was just serving at the local YMCA, serving at the local church and just really seeking God, you know. And I was really, really, really, really, really, really seeking God. I mean God had touched my life and I was just really hungry for God, you know, studying the Bible, anything I could get my hands on. I was there seeking God's will for my life, and just got really grounded in a great church and met some great friends and people.

I was at the YMCA one evening after working out in the gym and was chatting with the receptionist, Penny. One of the residents was applying for a new security officer role that had been created. This role had been created because lots of local kids were coming in and generally running riot.

Also most of the bodybuilders didn't pay to use the free weights and bodybuilding gym. Anyway, I was helping this resident with filling in his application form for the security officer job at Sheffield YMCA. When he had gone Penny asked why I didn't go for the job – I had a good grasp of what was wanted and she thought I would be perfect for it. I began to think about it.

The next time I was training at the gym, a lovely Christian lady, Viv, who was a fitness instructor, also encouraged me to go for the job, even though her husband was applying for it too!

I did apply for the job and got short listed. The interviews were with the then CEO Keith Wells and the company secretary Neville Chambers. That same week I got a hand-written letter, that I still have to this day, offering me the job. I wept as I read it, tears of appreciation and thanksgiving to God; he had answered my prayer and rewarded me for putting him first. The teachings of Christ that had first spoken to my heart years ago in Risley Remand Centre had come to pass:

But seek first his kingdom and his righteousness, and all these things will be given to you as well. (Matthew 6:33)

I now had a job in a good strong Christian organisation, adding value to people's lives. I was part of a great team of people with a great vision. I had a wonderful opportunity not just to look after the security of the building, but to look after the finance and any fire checks that needed to be done; and if there was an incident I was to go and defuse it. The staff was an interesting, colourful mixture of all kinds of faiths, shapes, sizes and cultures but at the core we were a Christian organisation that welcomed people of all faiths and none. I felt very valued for what I was doing; they appreciated me and it was a great opportunity for evangelism, to share my faith with the young people there, with the tenants there, with the staff there. And that's what

I did. I was also given the opportunity to organise programmes and events. With Dave Gilpin's leadership over me, I was very inspired by him. His style and his vision came upon my life. I began organising events, and got involved with local musicians to put on music evenings to bring the community together and to be able to share the Christian message. It was through this I started to develop a really good friendship with Herbie Armstrong. I also had opportunity to start my communication gift with the big crowds we started to get. I also took car, van and taxi loads of people to the alpha course. Many lives where changed through this life changing course, including mine.

I quickly settled into my job and took great delight in looking after the staff and users of the YMCA. I had to deal with the most challenging situations from breaking up fights with gangsters to calming down the young people who had come in to cause trouble. I befriended them and I really enjoyed my job.

One of my first jobs was to prioritise and clean up the bodybuilding gym. What I mean by this is by getting the people using it to pay! The massive bodybuilders were, in the majority, doormen or local gangsters. The good news was I had befriended most of the users of the gym as I worked out in the gym too. So, I strategically positioned myself in between the bodybuilding gym and the reception area where they were supposed to pay. The usual procedure was these huge, gift of the gab guys, would walk straight past reception, and the receptionists, supervisors and managers were too scared or intimidated to challenge them.

What I would do is politely greet them, often by name, ask them how their day had been. I offered to buy them a soft drink or coffee in the very upmarket restaurant. This approach really threw them! I would then say that I had to make sure everyone was a paid member, and they had to pay each time they came. I'm pleased to say that I managed over say a month, with the help of the reception staff, to get everyone to pay. Even guys who managed to get past me, I would politely say I needed a chat and, again, I would win them over and we would collect their money. Interestingly and wonderfully I became great friends with everyone! I even got invited out on the gangsters' birthdays! This was very funny – here's me, a full-on evangelist by now, devoted Christian, going out on the town for gangsters' birthday bashes. It was comical – these very well dressed cool cats, black, mixed race, white, very powerful men in every sense of the word, and I was a known associate! Only this time, I was praying, sharing what Jesus had done on the cross for them. I must say, this was a very exciting time. I trained with them whilst at the Bible college based in our church. My friends were really pleased and respected how I had changed my ways. I was accepted in my faith, my job, my church and with the ones Jesus seems to always have a heart for: the lonely, the marginalised, the criminal.

They say that if you do a job you like you never do a day's work in your life! That's how I felt with my new life. 2 Corinthians 5:17 says 'Therefore, if anyone is in Christ, the new creation has come: the old has gone, the new is here!'

Whilst doing my security and event-organising role I managed to get on a postgraduate management course. This was because there was a lot of management responsibility involved in the role. So here I was, now studying at postgraduate level when I had left school with no qualifications. This was truly amazing and very humbling and very challenging all at the same time.

Part of the excitement was I had to travel to London for study days at the George Williams College at Forest YMCA. George Williams was the founder of the YMCA, a former draper from Cornwall who went to London. Whilst in London he was converted to Christ. Walking home from church he said to his friend that if they could find seven selfless men they could change the world!

He started a prayer and Bible study above the draper's shop. Here, the young passionate George had a vision for a worldwide movement reaching and supporting people through programmes that helped them body, mind and spirit. This Christian charity, that welcomes all faiths and none, yet remained Christian at the core, soon took off. Lord Shaftesbury was the first president; a young Dr Bernardo soon joined this group of young evangelical philanthropists. Dr Bernardo went on to found the charity of his name to help all the young children and orphans sleeping under bushes less than ten minutes' walk from Lord Shaftesbury's residence. It was at a dinner party one evening that the petulant young doctor asked the question: 'Do you know that within a ten minute walk, many young children sleep out, under the bushes?'

Lord Shaftesbury answered, 'Let's put our silver knives and forks down and go and look.'

That night Dr Bernardo's was founded. Let's keep putting our silver down too and helping the less fortunate. In the Alpha course, Nicky Gumbel talks about these truly great young men and asks where are these great young men now? We need young men and women to be truly great and respond to the need around us, by faith, prayer and action. D.L. Moody, the great evangelist of around the same time, said, 'Be kind, conquer by love!'

So here I was studying at Sir George Williams College. It was a great honour. I did the four study days and then I also had four assignments to complete. I really studied hard and enjoyed the subject matter. It was all based around leadership and my role at the time. I graduated with distinction. I now had a postgraduate certificate in Management Studies under my belt. In one academic year I was more qualified than most of my peers! They say God has a sense of humour and he often uses weak and foolish people. I certainly qualified. 'Think of what you were when you were called. Not many of you were wise...' (1 Corinthians 1:26).

This first job was only part time, every night of the week from 6–10pm and all day Saturday. The job continued to grow as I continued to grow and then my boss, the company secretary, called me to the office. I got promoted from part time to full time. I was now working from 4–10pm Monday to Friday and all day Saturday. It was a perfect, tailor-made job for me. It utilised all the gifts God had put in me, but that had previously been used for the wrong reasons. My leadership gift had now been redeemed and restored to serve in the church and the local community.

I have some stories of incidents that occurred whilst working at SYMCA. A new guy started on the team; he was a black guy from the wrong side of the city in Sheffield. His street name was Budgie. On his first day – yes, his first day – it seemed like all hell broke loose at the YMCA. The reception I was talking about was in view and Budgie and I were getting to know each other over coffee. Bam, a black guy punched a thick-set white guy, then after much screaming he got another punch from a mixed-race guy. The next second it was like a boxing-cross-wrestling match. The girls on reception were screaming. Budgie followed my lead as I sped into action and began to calm the situation down. I managed to do this, but it was to have very serious repercussions!

The sports manager, unbeknown to me and without investigation, decided to ban the two known gangsters after chatting with the white doormen. I was at church one night, enjoying leadership training and prayer. At the end I turned on my mobile phone and found I had about seven voicemails from reception staff all the way up to CEO – could I come in for an emergency meeting? The church senior leaders all prayed for me and off I went.

I advised the CEO and senior management and then organised a meeting between the gangsters and the manager who had banned them; I would mediate. The gangsters had threatened to shoot the sports manager after his uninvestigated decision. After initial anger we banned all three for a month. I spoke to the white doorman and advised him of who he was disrespecting – he'd had no idea! The sports manager, who had once criticised me to my boss for spending too much time with these guys, thanked me for saving his life.

I had started Bible college now. It was perfect because Bible college was based at church and was every morning 9 a.m.–12 noon. I would then have a rest and prayer time at church, then go into the YMCA gym to workout, shower and then into work. I had now also moved into a flat of my own, near Claire my spiritual Mum. I started with a little flat and then I got Deke Rivers' flat. He was a guy who lived in the flat below mine and made a lot of noise as well as stealing mail. He got angry with me, called me a 'blankety blank' Christian, then ran and hid behind his door. I said he should thank God that I am 'blankety blank' Christian! Afterwards I read Luke 6 about loving your enemies and blessing and praying for them! This really helped shape my life and Christian character. Anyway, Deke was evicted for messing with the electricity and the landlord had to completely re-kit the flat and then I got it.

Around this time I heard Joyce Myers say this: 'Some of you think you're prophets to the nations and you can't even take authority over the dishes in your sink.' When I heard that I thought: Ouch!

From that day on I made a decision. I decided to wash up after every meal. It's had an amazing effect on my discipline. Take authority over small things. Reply to your emails. Do the paperwork. Hoover up. Get into the habit of being disciplined, and you'll be surprised what affect it will have on your relationship with Jesus. Jesus said if you rule over the small, he'll make you ruler over much more. Jesus tells us to start small.

In Zechariah 4:10 it says: 'Who dares despise the day of small things?' What that means is, don't underrate starting small. Everything has got to start somewhere. We all want big success and recognition. But a big oak tree comes from a small acorn. So don't get put off when you have to start from scratch. Abraham had nothing when he started out, called by God to leave his home for a new land promised by God – all he had was a promise from God, and his faith. Despite the fact that he and his wife were old, he became the father of a mighty nation.

When Joseph was sold into slavery by his brothers all he had was his God-given ability to interpret dreams. Using this gift, he rose from nothing to the position of chief adviser to the Egyptian pharaoh.

Peter was a lowly fisherman called by Jesus. Despite his failings and lack of education, his loyalty and faith in Jesus led him to become an inspirational leader of the apostles, a powerful speaker and writer. Jesus took Peter from his small beginnings to become the founder of his church.

I bought a brand new 50cc scooter and was now legally mobile for the first time since my mum bought me a moped when I was sixteen. I had also started to develop some great friends in church. One of these was a security manager for all the sports venues in Sheffield, including the Don Valley stadium. His name was Jeff Allott, a great guy, a real character. Jeff always had a smile on his face, was always joking, and we became good friends. He helped mentor me in the security world and also put me on the guest list for the Rolling Stones and UB40 (the reggae band with the same name as the card for signing-on for unemployment benefit). Here I was on the guest list for the Rolling Stones! The Bible talks about delighting yourself in the Lord and he will give you the desires of your heart. I was certainly being blessed, doors were opening for me; I was experiencing the favour of God in every area of my life.

Jeff said there was a one-bedroomed house for sale in his street – he lived in Treeton a quaint ex-mining village in Rotherham. It wasn't far from Sheffield, just a ten minute drive down the Parkway. The more I explored the house in Treeton, the more it opened up. I got the house for £27,000. The mortgage deal I got was £2,000 deposit with £2,000 cash back and the payments were well within my budget! Here I was buying my first house! It was very exciting. I had my own house with a lovely garden, parking space and a little palm tree in the garden. If they could see me now – I had bought a posh house on a posh estate! The main thing was, I was going on with my faith and I had great peace.

I decorated and moved into my house in Treeton. I also considered going to university to study some more. My family used to say to me, 'Terry, are you ready for this?' 'Do you think you'll be OK with a flat or a house?' 'Do you think you'll be OK at University?' They could not understand the faith I now had, leading four of them to Christ in that year: both of my sisters, one brother-in-law and my mum! It's also sad and amazing how those closest to us can't sort of let us start soaring like an eagle, you know; there's lots of promise to Christians in the Bible and I started to learn this really quick and how to appropriate them. But, anyway, I was just grateful every step of the way – I developed an attitude of gratitude; I was thankful for everything. If I could only be thankful for Jesus dying on a cross for me, that's enough for me, that really is enough, but it's much more than that, as I'll share.

I had been promoted to a housing support worker at Sheffield YMCA and this had management responsibilities. I also went to university and studied for a professional diploma in Management Studies. Again, this was exciting. It was hard but I learned how to manage my time well and, again, I graduated! This time all my new friends from church, who knew my story, came along and when my name was called out a big cheer went out! Terry Eckersley – Professional Diploma in Management Studies. Here I was now qualified as a housing professional. I had come a long way from the homeless section in Sheffield to now being qualified to work there or run it. God does have a sense of humour, hey? And he has no favourites – what he can do for one, he can do for all. If you have any needs like I had here's a good time to pause, reflect and pray, ask God to help you, to heal you, to provide for you. Remember Hebrews 13:8: 'Jesus Christ is the same yesterday and today and forever.' Jesus has called you to be a true apprentice. But is that what you want? Your local church leader can encourage you – that's great. Your boss can give you a great appraisal – that's great too. But nothing compares to affirmation from Jesus Christ. Nothing lasts like it. Everyone else has bad days but when you get affirmation from Jesus, you can take it to the bank. It's yours to keep forever.

Forgive and Be Forgiven

What small things can we give? Give forgiveness. It's a gift. And don't wait – give it now. Give forgiveness quickly and receive it quickly. If you don't receive it, if we carry guilt and bitterness around, we're making a mockery of what Jesus did on the cross. He died so that we can be forgiven.

It says in 1 John 1:9 'If we confess our sins [make a clean breast of them], he is faithful and just and will forgive us our sins and purify us from all unrighteousness.' So as soon as you've done something wrong – and you know it – repent quickly. Repenting is not about beating yourself up, it's about changing the way you think. But if you ask forgiveness you'll be cleaned. Simple as that! It becomes like you've never done anything wrong – you've been acquitted in heaven's courts. Now you're clean, pure, holy before God. Receive forgiveness and give forgiveness.

Learn to Fail Forwards

It's alright to fail doing something new, that's how you learn. The only person who never failed is someone who never tried anything. So it's OK to 'fail forwards'. Have a go. Try something new. Try new things in each area of your life. Get a new haircut, buy a new outfit – do something new and different.

God really blessed me in Sheffield and then, real interesting, the YMCA, which was an amazing place and had a great heritage in Sheffield, went through some huge financial challenges with capital funding and revenue funding being linked to that… I won't bore you. Many YMCAs then used the Housing Corporation Grant to subsidise the restaurant, etc. so the residents could get decent affordable meals. The Sheffield YMCA had to sell the whole building in order to keep sustainable and transfer everyone over to work for the university, apart from the housing department, of which I was one. It was phenomenal. The day that we got told about our redundancy God just really touched my life at home, and I knew that everything was fine, everything was going according to schedule. And on the last day I kept a sweet spirit. I was serving, helping to pack everything away, when a phone call came in the last ten minutes that I was there closing the place down. I picked it up and it was the regional executive from the Southern region, asking for me. I said, yes, it's Terry Eckersley speaking. She was asking would I like to come down for an interview for a housing manager's position at Southampton YMCA? They'd been through three housing managers in six months, the Chief Exec was on holiday, the housing manager had resigned – it was a mess. So, I said that I'd love to.

I drove down that weekend and stayed with my dear friends Herbie and Lisa Armstrong, and went for the interview. This was all happening so fast I didn't have time to be nervous!

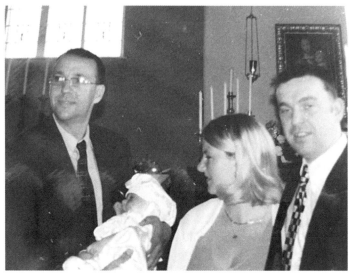

Proud day to be Godfather to Connor – Leanne and James' nephew

CHAPTER 13

Southampton YMCA And The South Coast: Smell The Sea Breeze

"There's nothing you can do that can't be done..."

JOHN LENNON

I met with the regional executive, she said, 'Terry, are you really, really sure about this?'

I said, 'Yeah, I'm fine about it.'

We prayed; I said, 'I'm fine about it.'

I met with the chairman who asked me a few questions on housing law. I'd done a professional diploma in housing, which was amazing as I'd left school with no qualifications at all. I'd learned all about housing law and policies and procedures, I'd been diligent in that.

He asked me questions on housing law and church life, and then said, 'You've got the job.'

'When do I start?' I asked.

'This afternoon!' he said. He suggested I stay for the week and then go home for the weekend and bring my stuff back. And that's what I did. I mean, talk about the suddenlys of God, that was absolutely phenomenal. And then I had to build, not physically with my hands because the housing project was there, but build a team, a structure and a system. I had half a member of staff, she was very small! Only teasing, she was part time, called Maria and she was a faithful woman of God. I said, 'Stand up, Maria.' She said, 'I am standing up!' Seriously, she was only small but she was a great lady.

Anyway, I had Maria and then all this government change came about with supporting people and contracts where you could charge for the support as well as the bricks and mortar. I got a team of seven and became very financially robust and healthy. I then went about recruiting my dream team. We had a mixed team, all great professionals and all life application faith-filled Christians. We started running Alpha courses there, Christian leadership – I mean we did work that was groundbreaking and phenomenal. I was in Andy Elmes' church, Portsmouth Family Church. He was a friend of mine; he'd preached in Sheffield and I'd met him when I'd looked after Herbie and Lisa's B& B and restaurant and music bar. It was just all perfectly fitted together. And Andy is not just a great friend and pastor, he is an amazing evangelist and a great man of God. I was under Andy's ministry for five years.

It was while I was on the south coast that I first got involved in the media and music industry. I've had twenty tracks played worldwide. Looping now, somewhere in the world ,there'll be some of my music playing on television on ITV's biggest-selling TV show *Monkey Business*, which is pretty phenomenal. I started that with no money – just a vision and a dream. I met a local movie director, Chris Barfoot, who had just been working with Prunella Scales, Shane Richie and Andrew Sachs. Chris was also working with Mark Hill, one half of The Artful Dodger, the famous UK 2Step Garage Godfather. Mark also co-wrote and produced Craig David's platinum selling albums and had four Ivor Novello awards. Celebrities of that era where coming from London just to be produced by Mark and use songs written by him or the stable of writers and producers he had signed to his label and publishing company.

I also met another guy who had had big success within the music industry, Barry Upton. Barry had been in Brotherhood of Man, the Eurovision winners and UK pop and chart act. He'd also written and worked with Stock, Aitken and Waterman. I must say, I read Pete Waterman's autobiography at the time and it is one of the best and most inspiring autobiographies I have ever read. Now, that's saying something as I have read hundreds of biographies of really inspiring business and Christian leaders.

So, Chris, Barry and I set up a company called Think Television and rented a small office. I was getting ideas for television shows, Chris would write the treatments and Barry would do the music for them. That was the idea. I also started meeting lots of other media types and got asked to do 'Thought for the Day' at the local BBC, so I was getting well known and networking around the media business in the evenings and at weekends. I still worked full time at the YMCA.

One of my friends from church, Tony Lister, a small balding northern guy who had a great sense of humour and was always clanging and punning, worked for the NHS in a drug relapse prevention unit. Tony wanted to make a DVD and wondered if I could help. I introduced him to another media friend of mine, Andy Sutton who's a cool media type, tall with a beard and great aspirations. He worked at the local ITV and also for a small production company. I helped Tony in the making of this DVD with my story and a few others who had beat addiction. I also had some backing tracks of some songs I had written and had them produced in an independent studio in Southampton. The DVD was a huge success. Whilst in its making, I asked Andy where he'd got the other background music from. He told me and then I suggested that the next time he needed music for anything I would supply it for him. A few weeks later he asked for some music for a pilot for a television series about a monkey rescue centre called *Monkey World*, led by Dr Alison Cronin and her husband. They rescued caged and mistreated monkeys from all over the world and then they helped them recover and breed at the already successful Monkey World.

I was delighted at the opportunity and asked Barry Upton if he wanted to get involved. I would write the music, he could produce it and I would then get it placed on this television show. He didn't need to think about it, it was too speculative and he would only work for pay. It's funny how some people think this way and lose out! I did let Andy use a couple of my tracks and in true form to my life, things started to happen very fast.

The series *Monkey Business* was bought by Discovery Channel International and I found myself writing and producing music for ITV's second largest-selling television show! What I had to do was recruit some friends – this was my strategy and plan of action. I would write, say, ten tracks, then give them to a budding producer to produce up according to the brief Andy would give me. One series would be Vietnamese sounding and titled music, the next could be African, from wherever location the show was being shot.

I recruited two main producers and also worked with one of Mark Hill's friends and producer Paul Tony Longland who had had some success primarily with songs. The other two guys were friends I had made at church and through my Christian network. These budding producers were Andy Bates, who first played Ebo (an effect you use to play the guitar – I first heard it on U2's 'With or Without You', a beautiful haunting melody) on a track I wrote called 'Give Me Grace', and Owen Wilkins who rented a room off a friend of mine.

The process worked. I often dropped tracks and when I picked them up passed them onto the exceptional editor Andy Sutton and thank God a lot of these tracks got placed on this ever popular show that was being shown all over the world. I saw this opportunity and I seized it with both hands. I would give the producers a 50/50 share on the writing royalty, that way we were all happy. I also had to setup a publishing company and signed these producers up to my publishing company, Think Media Music.

I also then saw the potential in putting these tracks onto the Internet as I sensed people would be using the Internet more and more rather than using CDs. I could give people the ease to search, sample and download tracks into whatever medium they wished, television to radio, wherever good music was needed. I started this in about 1998 and this library has grown and grown, and to date Think Media Music has six people signed to it. Andy Bates, who put a lot in in the early days, has decided to go his own way. I wish him well and every success.

I was at the YMCA National Conference a few years ago, around the *Monkey Business* time. My friend, another YMCA CEO, Danny Flynn, was leading it. This media company came and there was somebody there with credits from Sky BSB, ITV, Channel 4 and BBC. And I nudged Danny and said, 'We've got music on all those channels bar Channel 4, but we will have soon.' So, that's pretty amazing. And, again, I'm not glorying in my wisdom or my riches, I'm glorying in what God has done – it's pretty phenomenal. I learned lessons from significant Christian leaders and put them into practice in every area of my life. Success leaves clues. One person I have learned so much from is Corrie ten Boom and, like Claire Redhead, she deserves a mention in this book.

Thinking big on a trip to New York

CHAPTER 14

On The Job: Thank God For The Bed Bugs

Here come the sun, here comes the sun
It's all right, it's all right"

GEORGE HARRISON

I was learning and growing as a Christian and also as a professional. Yes, I did learn things from my ever increasing academic and professional studies, but I devoured biographies and learned the most from inspirational Christian leaders, one of whom was Corrie ten Boom.

Corrie ten Boom was a Christian Holocaust survivor from The Netherlands who helped many Jews escape the Nazis during World War II. She was an amazing lady with an amazing story. She said this: 'You never tap into the love of God as much as when you love your enemies.' So give it a go. If somebody wrongs you or says nasty things about you, learn to forgive them quickly. Pray for them and bless them. Send them a present or buy them a card. Then, as Corrie said, you can fully tap into the love of God. Corrie was sent to a concentration camp in World War II because her father had hidden Jewish people in his house. The family were grassed up by one of their friends. And Corrie's best friend had run off with her fiancé. She'd been hurt. Then she was sent to a concentration camp with her sister Betsy.

Corrie and her sister shared a cell at the camp. It stank. Their straw mattress was full of bugs and lice. Betsy was one of those enthusiastic Christians who really gets up your nose. She was always full of joy and peace. She was forever talking about 'the Lord and his word' and 'winning people for Christ', even when living in this hell on earth. Corrie asked her what they were going to do. Betsy told her not to be anxious, to give thanks and praise and make your request known to God. Corrie told her she'd taken it too far. She thought her sister was mad. They were in a concentration camp cell with a straw bed and lice. But Betsy said: 'Let's do it anyway, give thanks to God.'

So, they lifted their hands in that cell and praised God for who he was and thanked him because they had each other. Even for the straw bed. But Corrie told her sister she couldn't thank God for the bed bugs. Her sister replied: 'Why not?' So, reluctantly, Corrie joined her sister in thanking God for the bugs and lice.

Betsy died in the camp, but miraculously, due to an administration mix up, Corrie was released. She went on to become one of the most powerful evangelists ever. Corrie preached the word of God to thousands of people who were saved, healed and cleansed. Later, Corrie found out that every woman in the concentration camp had been brutally raped and abused by the prison guards. But she and her sister hadn't been raped because the guards wouldn't come in… because of the bed bugs. So, thank God for the bed bugs in your life! You don't know what they are keeping out. Learn to thank God for the hard times and you'll be anxious for nothing.

* * *

The work at Southampton YMCA became really interesting, the chief exec resigned and I became acting chief executive for about twelve months.

I was running things for a while and doing quite well, pushing out, getting into the community as well as running the housing and just raising leaders up all the time really, and growing the place, seeing people come to Christ. It was just fantastic.

And then I was interviewed for the chief executive role but didn't get it. It's important I tell you this story. Someone else got the chief executive role. And, Lord have mercy, have you ever worked for somebody who's controlling, or restricting, or all this, you know. It was just like that, I mean I couldn't believe it. And then it went from bad to worse; someone there accused me of some pretty nasty stuff, you know, that I wasn't being due diligent, which I was. I won't bore you with the details, but there were some pretty nasty allegations being made against me.

So, my great friend John Bradwell dropped everything – that's what great friends do – he dropped everything and supported me in that, I mean amazingly. John's got a great legal background in his history. I called him George Carmen QC. George Carmen QC was one of the greatest QCs this nation has ever seen. He did some of the best cases, and won! But I had George Carmen by my side and, John, bless him, I mean he'd tell this story better than me, but I was forgiving my accuser, blessing him, doing good to him, doing everything I could… and perhaps going too far. ButJohn said that no, we've got to really stand on this, we're fighting to the hilt.

I agreed to John's advice, but behind the scenes was living the Jesus style! This next scripture had jumped off the page one night, and I knew it was something I would have to apply to my life.

> But to you who are listening I say: love your enemies, do good to those who hate you, bless those who curse you, pray for those who ill-treat you. If someone slaps you on one cheek, turn to them the other also. If someone takes your coat, do not withhold your shirt from them. Give to everyone who asks you, and if anyone takes what belongs to you, do not

demand it back. Do to others as you would have them do to you.

If you love those who love you, what credit is that to you? Even sinners love those who love them. And if you do good to those who are good to you, what credit is that to you? Even sinners do that. And if you lend to those from whom you expect repayment, what credit is that to you? Even sinners lend to sinners, expecting to be repaid in full. But love your enemies, do good to them, and lend to them without expecting to get anything back. Then your reward will be great, and you will be children of the Most High, because he is kind to the ungrateful and wicked. Be merciful, just as your Father is merciful.

Why do you call me, 'Lord, Lord,' and do not do what I say? As for everyone who comes to me and hears my words and puts them into practice, I will show you what they are like. They are like a man building a house, who dug down deep and laid the foundation on rock. When the flood came, the torrent struck that house but could not shake it, because it was well built. But the one who hears my words and does not put them into practice is like a man who built a house on the ground without a foundation. The moment the torrent struck that house, it collapsed and its destruction was complete.
(Luke 6:27–36, 46–49)

I have continued to apply this, by quality decision and this has brought continued victory and Christian character to my life. The old me has wanted to do the opposite, by the grace of God I have managed to apply the above.

And, after a long story cut very short – the other side were apologising, backtracking and I got, you know, delivered, vindicated, whatever you want to call it. It was great. At the end of it all, or in between, we prayed together and just declared the truth of God's word and blessing, and the presence of God just invaded my room in Southampton, And we knew, we knew that God was up to some amazing stuff behind the scenes, as always, you know.

I went on a reconciliation meeting with the person who'd levelled these allegations, and it all came out – and this may help some of you – that he'd done it because he was jealous of me. He confessed it. He said, 'I'm sorry, Terry, before we move on, I've got to say I was just very, very jealous of you.' Isn't it an amazing thing what jealousy can do? But, it's an amazing thing that God is bigger than anything; God is bigger than any allegation, he's bigger than any opposition, God is absolutely huge.

I stayed there for a few more months, but I'd seen a chief exec's role advertised. I put my CV together and sent it off really quick. I'd almost forgotten I'd done it because in this period as well I'd had a vision about getting into TV and media. I'd had this vision about writing this book and another book, so these things were happening, and I was just very, very fruitful. I believe God was starting to talk to me as I was becoming very, very rich, a very successful entrepreneur. Everywhere I went I was just getting this spoken into me, you know, and flicking my switch, and I was reading and praying, and just really getting a load of entrepreneurial stuff going.

So, all this started taking off, and I was just managing the YMCA stuff, just spinning on my head, you know, I'd really outgrown it. Then I got a call from another regional exec of the YMCA inviting me for an interview for a chief executive position in Woking. So, I went along. As she spoke on the phone I felt the touch of God on it, that's what I call it, I just felt the presence of God. When God speaks to me I just weep under his presence. I felt God was leading me there. I went for one interview, went back for a second interview and, long story short, they offered me the job, which was amazing!

Lives changed at Surrey YMCA

Terry with Dominic Monaghan
("Show me the Funny" winner)

CHAPTER 15

It Sounds Like A Long Way,
It's Within Woking Distance

"I know you haven't made your mind up yet
But I would never do you wrong I've known it from the
moment that we met
No doubt in my mind where you belong"

DYLAN

———

What was really amazing was that the Local Borough Council had given the YMCA a brand new property, hardly touched, two floors, on a twenty-five year lease with a peppercorn rent, maybe a grand a year, and £750,000 to refurbish one floor. Right, that's pretty exciting!

The other amazing thing was, there was no office, no systems, no structures, no treasurer, no finance, no plan – there was absolutely nothing. But there was a vision and I had a calling from God. I remember going there on my first day and this guy said that he'd take me to my office. It was a portakabin behind a Methodist church – bless them, they let us use it to start with. There was no desk, there was no phone, it was just this empty room.

I wondered what on earth I'd let myself into? I had a mobile phone, about seven names and addresses… that's it. I thought, I've got to start somewhere! I called Janet Webb, who had been like a spiritual mum to me, and we prayed on the phone.

I was invited to go on holiday with Janet and her husband Stan later that year, along with their son Nick and beautiful daughter Jill, who by now was getting used to putting up with this strange guy, who talked a lot and fell asleep after meals at her home. I leapt at the chance. We went to Malta and had a great time with the family. I started to spend some time with Jill alone, going for walks and coffees and chats.

Anyway, so I started going down the list. I just wanted to meet people and network. I had a great Christian Chairman, Les Taylor, and a great faithful board, but what I really loved was that yes, it was a challenge. George Williams, who founded the YMCA, when he received his OBE he said to the whole YMCA movement, 'Many things have been wrought by faith and prayer, never underestimate the potency of your personal example and continue to win people for Christ.' He gave the movement three keys, that's all we really need in life: faith and prayer, potency of our example, and lead people to Christ. It's a recipe for success; it's all we need – three keys.

So, part of me thought, wow, I can be a D.L. Moody, you know, I can be a Sir George Williams, this is great. So, I started on my list, started meeting with Christian leaders, council leaders, anybody and everybody in the town who worked with young people and YMCA community associated stuff.

I was in temporary accommodation when I first moved there. I'm going to tell you this story, and this is the way I live my life now. As somebody once said, how can you walk on water if you don't step out of the boat, right? Now it's easy to say that as a preacher, isn't it? You just say it. But to live it is a challenge. The beautiful thing is that when God calls you to step out of the boat, he'll sustain you as long as you keep your eyes on him. And, it's just a different level of living. It's awesome when things are so big and so huge for you, you've got to rely on God, you've got absolutely no alternative, you've got to rely and trust on

God. In Luke, in The Message translation, Jesus said that if we want to be his true apprentice, not Alan Sugar or Trump, if we want to be his true apprentice, we'll do these things. He says the work is huge that he's called us to, but to rely on him. And as I rely on the Lord, I've learnt to really cast my cares on him, which I've done all my Christian life, because he cares for me. So everything, no matter how huge it is, I refuse to keep hold of any cares. Like David said in Psalm 23, 'I shall not want.' I shall not want, I refuse to carry any cares.

So, I'm listing all these cares before the Lord. How am I going to get revenue funding? Everybody was telling me I couldn't do it. How could I do this, how could I do that? I'm just listing it all before the Lord. And I went to a meeting at a church where they wanted my advice on youth work. They started with this beautiful song about the power of the cross; everything was met at the cross, and I started weeping in the presence of God.

Then this guy got his Bible and shared this – and I'm going to quote this to you, this is really powerful:

> So he said to me, 'This is the word of the LORD to Zerubbabel: 'Not by might nor by power, but by my Spirit,' says the LORD Almighty.
> (Zechariah 4:6)

I had heard that and understood it.

> What are you, mighty mountain? Before Zerubbabel you will become level ground. Then he will bring out the capstone to shouts of 'God bless it! God bless it!'
> (Zechariah 4:7)

I'd heard that. This is Zerubbabel rebuilding the Temple of God.

Then the word of the LORD came to me: 'The hands of Zerubbabel have laid the foundation of this temple; his hands will also complete it. Then you will know that the LORD Almighty has sent me to you.'
(Zechariah 4:8–9)

And God spoke to me through that scripture and, from that day to this, I kept on that promise of God. Deep within me I knew that I was going to complete building Woking YMCA.

Terry's early songwriting days at first flat.

Terry at the BBC Media Centre in Salford, talking Dreams and Visions with Barry Woodward

Charlie Hale – a friend of mine, with Mike Tyson

Big adventures ahead in Sheffield

CHAPTER 16

Challenges – Including Steve Jobs Victory!

"Let it be, let it be…"

PAUL MCCARTNEY

W e completed the first floor of Woking YMCA. It was more than financially viable. We got more programmes than anybody in Surrey. (I nearly said the UK – I don't want to be evangelastic!) We were doing so much it was phenomenal. Woking YMCA has got about ten paid members of staff and lots of volunteers and interns on the books.

Things just kept increasing as I kept just turning up at my now new office in the completed Youth Development Centre called the Ypod. We were gaining national notoriety – we'd had visits from Deputy Prime Minister Nick Clegg! We were used as one of four centres in the UK, by the National Youth Agency, as a case study for BIG capital funded youth programmes! Things kept growing as we had leadership training every month and every week for those we were developing as senior managers.

However, I must warn you! Pioneering was like cutting through steel – this was from everything from our bank account, to funding applications – there will be opposition to your mission. I told you about the name Ypod. This came about because we ran a competition about the name and a young lady chose Ypod – we loved it! We had a recording studio, Internet cafe and drop in centre, youth apprenticeships, gig nights, alternative education for excluded schoolchildren and those on the verge of exclusion, dance classes, church for youth on Sundays – wow, lives were getting changed, powerfully.

Then I got a call from Steve Jobs' top lawyer in the UK. Apple, the computer and phone company, were not happy that we'd called our centre the Ypod! He said we were diluting their brand! I thought and said, 'C'mon, why not give us some iPods and we can run a competition for young people! We are a charity, helping them.'

The lawyer wasn't convinced. I was angry that they were giving us this unfounded opposition. I even went to meet the lawyer at Canary Wharf in London. I was with my gracious, wise chairman, Les Taylor, and we were ushered into the big lawyer's office. They said again that we were diluting their brand. I politely pointed out that, after much research, Apple only had the copyright on the name 'Pod' for software, music and computers, not youth development centres. I posed the question: if we converted some old toilets and called them the Pee Pods, would they still be on my case?

We crossed swords time and time again.

We both could see that this lawyer would have to report back to someone. We had not yet consulted a lawyer; the board trusted us to handle it. They instructed me to write to Apple's CEO Steve Jobs! So, here I was CEO Terry Eckersley, writing to CEO Steve Jobs (this was after the iPhone phenomena but not yet up to the iPhone three, four or five). This was annoying for me although I had kept my decision to live happy and thankfully on purpose, I wouldn't let this put me off.

Anyway, long story short, after lots of letters and faxes between Steve Jobs and myself, we finally won! Steve Jobs and the Apple giant lost against the small David, Terry Eckersley and the Christian charity the YMCA. I was very happy. I studied the life and death of Steve Jobs years later and have so much respect for the guy.

Everything changes…

There had been so many changes in my life, and one of the biggest and best was the change in my relationship with Jill – Janet's daughter.

Jill came to serve at the YMCA in Woking where I was CEO. It was amazing that I had known Jill over ten years, but now she was seeing me in a different light. We were getting on really well; we would chat regularly on the phone and I would go up north to see her (not just the family); we'd go out for meals and we were getting closer. By now I had become very successful and had all the trappings. I had bought a BMW sports car and a flat in Surrey.

We'd placed an advert with the local Woking churches for accommodation for Jill as a 'volunteer young woman at the Woking YMCA'. We'd been relying on this advert to get Jill a place to stay. Time was running out and I was just typing an email to another YMCA that provided housing, giving the dates she would be volunteering in the hope of getting her somewhere to stay, when I got a phone call from a local Christian couple who had a room for her. This couple had a large, detached mansion and three spare rooms! They gave the room at no charge and became good friends to Jill and myself.

Jill served on team at Woking YMCA and we were starting to fall in love. Jill had seen another side to me as I had dropped everything to visit her very sick mother Janet. This was a tremendous time for both of us, but equally challenging. We had known each other so long like sister and brother, now it was all changing and we didn't want to get it wrong or hurt each other. Jill and I were both praying about this and I knew that God was giving me a green light.

Our first date was when I was invited to Buckingham Palace in recognition of the work I had done in the community. I was able to have someone accompany me and Jill's mum, Janet, who was like one of my best friends and had become like a spiritual surrogate mother, hinted heavily that I should take Jill. So I asked if she would like to come and she said yes! We went through the formalities of security and being commanded by the Lord Lieutenant to attend the Queen's Garden Party at Buckingham Palace.

It's also challenging to recall not long later we where to nurse Janet through a three month battle with a brain tumour before she had a vision of Jasper, the foundation stone of heaven before she went to be there. Claire joined her not long later.

Dreams come true

I proposed to Jill just off Bond Street in London, after a sort of work review! Jill was so surprised she was laughing in shock and I said, 'You'd better make your mind up; we're booked into Tiffany's just around the corner.' Jill picked her engagement ring from her favourite jewellers and in less than nine months we were married.

I had a one-bedroomed flat that we moved into after an amazing wedding. The first thing I did was buy Jill a new kitchen. I did the same as I did with Tiffany's – I gave her a budget and then let her pick. And I must say what an amazing homemaker Jill is with her background in home furnishings at Laura Ashley and her own amazing styling.

Back to the wedding, we had a great celebration with our friends. The wedding was everything Jill wanted. We got married in a beautiful Old Village Church in Woking. Jill had sung at so many weddings that were almost a contemporary Christian conveyer belt that we both wanted to be married the traditional way. We had a great service. I arrived on a motor bike and side car, as did my best man John Bradwell. He looked very nervous which was funny as he is a well built, typical mans man! So did my ushers, Dr Nick Tiffin, a top consultant pathologist and dear friend, and Wayne Leigh, an incredible charismatic businessman. Wayne met and greeted all at the church. We had a beautiful dream, sun-filled, love- and faith-filled marriage. I was marrying the woman of my dreams and best friend. After the service we then went to a local hotel for the wedding breakfast. Everyone who came was intrinsically a part of our journey, an encouragement and support to all we had become. I covered this in my Groom's speech which was part stand up comedy, part evangelist giving glory to God and his people who had been so significant in both our lives. By now I had spoken all over the UK and the world. In Churches, Schools, Prisons, Conferences, Business meetings, in fact anywhere I get invited. Always bearing much fruit.

Everything's gonna be alright!

So much was happening. I managed to recruit Paul Weller from The Jam as a patron of the YMCA, along with another local philanthropist Chris Ingram, who is also the president of Shelter. He sold one of his companies for half a billion! Yes, half a billion. I became great friends with Chris who even gave me a vintage signed-by-a-celebrity bottle of champagne. Chris is a very good man. He also later supported us in other ways which I will never forget.

Things kept growing and growing and growing, people kept growing and growing and growing.

Then one afternoon I checked the bank balance: we only had £350 in the bank. This was serious, we now had a lot of staff, we had a children's centre in our building and lots of other charities. Thankfully this was just before a holiday, the pressure was becoming intense.

Jill and I set off for sunny Spain to spend some time at our timeshare. We have had great holidays twice sometimes three times a year. I've been fortunate and travelled all around the world, some trips Jill and I did together, some before we got married. I've visited USA, Germany, Paris France (to celebrate our engagement), Canary Islands, Sweden. I have taken young people to Strasbourg to see the

European Parliament. I led young people on a YMCA Tensing trip in Norway (where the big 1980s band A-Ha came from!). I've also been to Kiev on a short term mission and speaking trip to Hillsong Ukraine. I had a girlfriend in Ukraine: she was a chick in Kiev! (Sorry.)

This time we went to Spain and the pressure was intense. For weeks I had printed off and was speaking and praying all of Gods promises on provision. I had also devoured Hudson Taylor's book on how he founded the CIM (China Inland Mission) on faith and prayer alone! I was still getting no relief. We enjoyed the holiday, swam, had time by the pool, ate in, ate out – intense pressure, failure, fear were banging and screaming at my door. I was spending time alone in prayer, nothing was shifting. We settled down one night to watch a DVD called Letters to God.

This film is based on the true story of Tyler Doherty, an extraordinary eight-year-old boy who faces his daily battle against cancer with bravery and grace. He is surrounded by a loving family and community, and is armed with the courage of his faith. To Tyler, God is a friend, a teacher and the ultimate pen pal. Tyler's prayers are his letters to God which he posts on a daily basis. The letters find their way into the hands of Brady McDaniels, the substitute postman with a troubled life of his own. He is confused over what to do with the letters but becomes entangled in the boy's family and journey when he reads them. They inspire him to seek a better life for himself.

This film really spoke to me – it was as if the world stopped and the emotions of the characters in the film were how I was feeling. I cried out to God angrily, 'God you're supposed to be my loving father and I feel lonely, angry and abandoned!'

Suddenly, the whole room filled with the presence of God. I was weeping once more under the comforting presence of the Holy Spirit. I knew that everything was gonna be alright, and maybe this is applicable to you right now. Get real with God and he will answer you in a very real and tangible way. I had been doing everything I could do to try and help God – casting my care, praying, confessing provision scriptures – and yes, this is all great. However, at the end of the day and the start of the day, his mercy is new and everything comes by faith and prayer and surrender!

I shared with Jill. Everything's gonna be alright, I told her. God Almighty had touched me. I felt as light as a feather. Everything was gonna be OK, even though we had only £350 in the YMCA bank account!

We now had a great holiday, enjoying time by the pool, in the sea and on the beach, meals out in a local tapas café. We managed to squeeze in a few shopping trips for Jill who always needs more shoes and handbags! I'm only teasing; Jill always comments that my wardrobe's much fuller than hers. I nod and smile. I always have the last word in our house… yes dear!

We had a tremendous holiday and were soon travelling back. I love flying and I love travelling around the world – I feel like this is what I was born for.

I went back to work at my office based at the now thriving Ypod Centre. I had a coaching session with a great friend of mine, Rich Thorby. I was being a guineapig for him in a weighty academic coaching course he was now doing after a successful business career as a commercial CEO. I'd met him at Hillsong Church London. Rich was also on the board of a major international ministry, Derek Prince. Although Derek has passed away, his teaching is still relevant and applicable for today.

Back to Rich: Rich is a deep thinker, caring, meticulous, his cogs are always going, he's very intelligent and articulate. He started to coach me: 'Do you have one major challenge we can look at?' I shared the naturally impossible financial problem we had of only £350 in the bank. However I was in faith and shared this with Rich. We talked about what we could do naturally speaking – chase bad debt, etc. – and then packed up for the weekend. Naturally speaking we should have closed the project but thankfully my chairman at that time, Adrian Fortescue, was also in faith; we knew there had to be more!

I had a voicemail on Saturday morning. It was from Lynne Coutts, the lovely ex YMCA training executive who I'd employed to work for me two days a week fundraising. I rang her back full of expectation. She was overjoyed as she told me, and I wept tears of joy and relief; we had won £500,000 funding for all costs for five years! This was the manifestation of the miracle. Thank God for his faithfulness as we follow and trust him!

Grove Court

Next was a brand new 24-bed housing project I'd been working towards with the local council and another Christian charity, Shelter.

I had been meeting sporadically with the chairman of a local housing charity. He knew I had a great relationship with local councillors and the CEO of the council, the charismatic, big-thinking Ray Morgan. Ray had overseen the development of Woking and had become a good friend, still political, but a dear friend. He had made Woking a world leader in all things green in the UK and all around the world. This also brought much jealousy and opposition. WARNING! Success brings many things including – what I find hard to understand – jealousy! Ray, like me, had his fair share of critics! I have to forgive and bless them – so, I do – and I'm gonna try and not mention them. Bless them, Lord, they know not what they do!

So, I had a call from the local council and the housing charity, and we were offered a chance to start developing plans for a shared housing project. I ran this by the board who were, in majority, in favour of taking this project forwards. I had visited the building which was a brand new complex of flats (like penthouse pads!) with a new chairman. We prayed outside in my car and the presence of God filled the whole car, so we were very convinced ('fully persuaded' the Bible calls this in Romans 4). One member of the board was very angrily opposed to the project. Worryingly, they were later to become Chair after continuously challenging the new chair. (He later developed cancer.

We prayed together and by the grace of God he was healed.)

The head of children's services wanted two bed spaces and would pay £30K a year. Things were going from glory to glory. We soon had this housing project up and running! We got all free beds from YMCA England. Provision just kept coming and coming and we soon had £50K in reserves and a very strong team continuing to develop. James Alexander, a lovely guy, who had come to me via a local lawyer, hurting from a bad employment experience, was now running the housing project very successfully.

Surrey Youth Consortium

Woking YMCA gained £500,000 funding from the Lottery and then shortly afterwards a housing project with the local Council and County Council and another Christian Charity. We also won a bid of 10 more youth centres with about 300 seconded staff from the Surrey County Council!

I remember going to Woking and praying that I wanted to influence great leaders in and around Woking and Surrey, and the UK. And now I'm influencing key Muslim figures in the UK, in relationship with them, and sharing the gospel of Jesus Christ through amazing doors and opportunities. I'm influencing guys at top level in government, I'm influencing church leaders. I mean, amazing, I could share some names with you which just like blow my mind!

I also got involved in bringing one of the world's leading brands into the UK: it's the second largest coffee company in the world and they give to compassion and mercy ministries at all levels. It was amazing how that door opened. My wife Jill gave me a contact and then I met the guy. I told him that I was the man, for sure, to help him roll this out in London and the south of England. I just wanted to serve the vision. Through this, I'm meeting some incredible people in spheres of influence, so I'm really leading in four levels, in overseeing four things. If Richard Branson can do it, why can't I? You know, if Donald Trump can do it, why can't you do it? If the lady from Body Shop, Anita Roddick, who I met, can do it, why can't you do it? Think about it. If we are Christians we've got the gifting and the power of the Almighty God. Remember the utmost level: they're just living at the most level; we can live at the utmost level. One of my role models and mentors Tim Storey coined this phrase: 'An utmost God wants us to live utmost lives!' I believe it.

Somebody said to me, 'How do you do all this, Terry?'

I asked, 'Does Richard Branson fly planes?'

He said, 'No.'

I told him, 'You don't need to fly the planes; you can train other people to fly the planes.'

It's about time that we had some Christian philanthropists and entrepreneurs rise up in the UK 'for such a time as this'. If Cadbury can do it through chocolate, why can't Terry Eckersley do it through media music?

When I was at Portsmouth Family Church this word got right in my heart and my spirit, and I suggest that you write it down, you study it and you put it at the bottom of every prayer that you pray. Paul was talking to the church in Ephesus about the grace – and he knelt before them, and he prayed for them that God's love would fill them, and they would know how wide and long and high and deep the love of Christ is.

But then he says, he's done his best, he's prayed his greatest. He says, 'Now to him who is able to do immeasurably more than all we ask or imagine, according to his power that is at work within us' (Ephesians 3:20). So, the 'according to' is like my car: its speed is according to the power I put down on the accelerator. And it's the same with God: according to how much power you're letting him work in your life, according to your belief and faith level – God's not putting a lid on your life, he's able to do immeasurably more than all we ask or imagine.

It's time we started asking again, it's time we started imagining again. The Bible speaks about witty inventions. I know this guy called Wayne Leigh. I mean, come on, if you want to be inspired go and talk to this guy for five minutes. He has invented coat hanger pens, he has laser pens, you name it he has it. He's also such a funny guy, a natural salesman and Bruce Willis lookalike since he's gone bald! He's got six kids, a great wife called Adele. He runs a successful promotional gifts business. Should he work hard? Should we? Absolutely, but he's yielded his imagination and his gifting to God. There are no limits or constraints on our lives, only the ones we put on them. I have Andy Elmes to thank who was my Pastor for five years whilst on the south coast.

Even what you've done up to date, it's nothing. God's able to do immeasurably more. This is not for us to be selfish – no, we can bless people. We can live to be a blessing. How many poor people do you know? How many broke people do you know? How many people could you help and encourage if God blessed you? I'm not just talking about finance, but about peace and prosperity of soul, lasting prosperity, health, you know, joy, motivation, being a giver rather than a taker.

> God sets the lonely in families, he leads out the
> prisoners with singing; but the rebellious live in
> a sun-scorched land. (Psalm 68:6)

Anybody who's lonely, God sets you in families. God set me in the Redhead family, such a Godly mother of the family Claire – the closest to Jesus I have met in skin. God set me in the Webb family through my relationship with Janet. All the single guys in the church fancied her daughter who was the beautiful worship leader. She sang and looked like an angel. And when God sets you, he sets you; it's like a diamond in a ring. When the jeweller sets a diamond in a ring, he sets it, but that diamond's also going to shine in that ring. It's like everything with God, it's mutually beneficial. We've all got so much to offer, it's so great. Why not get involved in a local church, support the local church, get involved in a local charity that's on your heart, you know, serve them, serve people, let the joy of God just impact other people through your life.

Jill at Silencio Church Tenerife

Brothers reunited – Stan the preacher man

"True Apprentice" at my dear friend & fellow evangelist JJohn at UK Evangelists conference

Three Musketeers. My two brothers James and John.

CHAPTER 17

Looking to the future

"The story of life is quicker than the wink of an eye, the story of love is hello and goodbye... until we meet again"

JIMI HENDRIX

I have been planted in three locations and three local churches and have travelled a million miles from my life of drugs and crime.

I haven't mentioned Hillsong London and the exceptional leadership team of Bevan Russell, Kris Mikkelson, and the senior leader Gary Clarke. I have so much to thank this team for not to mention the senior leader Brian Houston.

Jill and I now own a flat and a detached old railway cottage which we bought in 2010. It has lovely old beams and is at the bottom of a private drive – a long way from the council estate I thought I would never leave. Jill has made this into a beautiful home.

Despite the double-dip recession I have built the YMCA to completion! We are now waiting on the Lord to see the rest of his blueprint plan for our lives. We are still doing as we are waiting. We are planted in a great local Church. We also are visiting three countries in the next three months speaking in Churches, helping people and appearing on Radio & Television. This and another book are being released. To facilitate this we are setting up another Charity that helps other people all around the world. As we do, we pray that you will also find God's pleasing and perfect will for your lives, as you trust and wait on him. God has a unique personalised plan for your life.

We are always looking to the future. As we established earlier, it's always good to deal with worry, or worry will continually deal with us. In this next chapter of our lives and ours its so important to dream big and take small steps. This was a strapline I used in one of the many companies I have founded, led and ran.

So please, let's all dream. And action, we have just started to found and lead as CEO of a new international charity, called Think International Enterprises. This is the first steps mission statement;

Overview

- To serve, strengthen & help all people & people groups all around the world.
- To be diligent in supporting the Nations, environment and communities especially the the most vulnerable, needy and marginalised.
- Supporting credible Charitable organisations and staff with buildings, technology, training, funding and coaching.
- Serving and strengthening National & International Initiatives within legal and moral constraints.
- We welcome ALL people's of ALL faiths and none.

As you can see, we are dreaming huge! We are helping with lobbying about homelessness and education, sex trafficking and drug abuse, training and employment. You name it. Therefore we can help as many people as possible in the world with need. Most people fall into this category, I do! So, lets start with a servant heart in mind, and get our eyes of our own needs and get lost in he needs of others, as we have determined.

We also have lots of other speaking and serving opportunities at the time of writing. Just next week, we have a speaking engagement in a NHS detoxification ward, followed by an interview on a national radio show. We are also meeting with a leader from Uganda called Dr Daniel Nkata who has 300 organisations he want us to help, we are meeting with him in Luton. He was on the welcome team when another well known Evangelist called Reinhard Bonkke, when he did some speaking in Uganda.

After that we are travelling to an island off darkest Africa called Tenerife! We are doing about four meetings myself and a great friend called Reverend Davey Falcus, please read his book *Gangland to God* and be inspired. Talking of Davey we have just helped him get two buildings and also helping another YMCA CEO in Newcastle with leadership and funding.

When back from Tenerife we are then going to Bulgaria taking aid, gifts and hope to orphanages and Churches out there. Life is rich, full and exciting. I'm doing all this with my beautiful wife, whom I love more and more each day we spend together, my other family and friends. Doing life with those who celebrate you, not just tolerate you.

I'm not saying all this to impress you, as with the rest of the book, I'm saying it to impress upon you, you too have a mighty purpose and we can always get our bounce back. I continue to time and time again. So can you. If you have your bounce in life, please help others, everything else gets selfish and unfulfilling.

As you can see, there are many new and exciting adventures on the horizon. I sense this is the case not just for me, but you also. I'm glad we connected and now are friends, please keep in touch. It won't be that long before we both have much more to report. We were after all both born ready!

'Inspirational' Terry looking for a fresh start after YMCA exit

by John Ellul

Terry Eckersley with the Liberal Shadow Home Secretary Nick Clegg in 2007.

Terry Eckersley, centre, pictured with Graffiti artist Mister Boilem, left and music producer Mark Hill at the Y

Looking to the future...

Terry with good friend & member of pastoral team at Hillsong London 2009 Mark "Wilko" Wilkinson

At Hillsong

Further information

Why not book Terry for an event he is available to speak at: Church Services, School lessons, Assemblies, Youth Events, Dinners, Business Meetings, Breakfasts, Conferences. The speaking has been accompanied by many conversions and healing experiences. Terry has travelled to four continents speaking in Churches of all denominations as well as Schools, Business meetings, Youth Events, Prisons, Stadiums, Bible schools, Conferences as well as Radio, TV, Satellite TV.

To contact Terry, email him at at terryeckersley@me.com. For latest news and events visit www.terryeckersley.co.uk

To order more copies of Born Ready, order online at www.veriteshop.co.uk or phone Verité on 01903 241975

Born Ready Prayer

Dear loving God.

Thank you that Jesus died so we may have ALL we need for life & Godliness.

I'm sorry I have done wrong, thanks for your forgiveness.

I'm now born ready for ALL life has for me!

Fill me with your Spirit.

Amen.